P9-AOG-238

The Rescue and Romance
Popular Novels Before World War I

The Rescue and Romance
Popular Novels Before World War I

Diana Reep

Bowling Green State University Popular Press
Bowling Green, Ohio 43403

Copyright © 1982 Bowling Green University Popular Press

Library of Congress Catalog Card No.: 82-061169

ISBN: 0-87972-211-8 Clothbound
      0-87972-212-6 Paperback

To my father, Howard Reep

Contents

Preface

My study of the rescue motif in popular American novels before World War I focusses on the rescue convention as part of the romantic plot of the novels. The rescue as a structured convention which controls the movement of the romantic plot appears in all types of popular novels. It appears in domestic novels, in gothics, in dime novels, in historical romances and in westerns. It is used by writers as disparate as Edward Ellis and Susan Warner. It is present at the introduction of the novel as a genre and continues to appear in popular novels of this day.

For this study I used some fifty novels. I am indebted to the works of Alice Payne Hackett, James D. Hart and Frank Luther Mott for the titles of bestselling novels or titles by consistently popular writers before World War I. I was concerned less about the total sales of the novels than about whether the books easily fit the definition of popular works or are the works of writers who sold well over a long period of time. The early American novels that I have used were surpassed on sales lists by British novels of the time. But I have examined these novels, written before Cooper's main work, because they are part of the development of the American popular novel.

Chapter I

The Rescue

In 1853 Nathaniel Hawthorne received $144.09 in royalties for *Mosses From an Old Manse*. Also in 1853 Henry David Thoreau learned from his publisher that his *Week on the Concord and Merrimack Rivers* had sold only 219 copies since its 1849 publication. These figures, however, were not indicative of a terrible slump in the American publishing business. In that same year, Susan Warner got $4,500 for six months' sales of *The Wide, Wide World*. And Fanny Fern sold 70,000 copies of *Fern Leaves from Fanny's Portfolio*.

The next year, a novel about a poor orphan girl who is befriended by a kindly lamplighter and later taken into the home of a warm-hearted blind woman, where, years later, she is discovered by her long lost father (now wealthy) sold 40,000 copies within the first eight weeks of publication.[1] *The Lamplighter* is one of the reasons Hawthorne exploded with his well-known comment about the "damned mob of scribbling women":

> What is the mystery of these innumerable editions of the *'Lamplighter'* and other books neither better nor worse?—worse they could not be and better they need not be, when they sell by the 100,000.[2]

Actually, Hawthorne's competition was not just a few scribbling women. Many women found writing popular novels a good way to make money, but so did many men. Hawthorne's competition was a sizeable group of writers who apparently knew precisely what the public wanted to buy. Sylvanius T. Cobb, for example, wrote 122 novels from 1850 to 1873—they all sold very well. Timothy Shay Arthur's *Ten Nights in a Barroom: and What I Saw There* (1854) sold 100,000 copies a year for twenty years. George Lippard and E.Z.C. Judson (Ned Buntline) wrote lurid novels about vice in the cities—and had great success. E.D.E.N. Southworth (the "Queen" of the domestic novel) sold 200,000 copies of her first novel,

3

Retribution (1847) and wrote sixty-one more novels, all successful.[3] What really frustrated Hawthorne was the question of what made this fiction so enormously popular.

This same question has interested critics such as John Cawelti, Russel Nye, James Hart, Frank Luther Mott and Ray Browne, all of whom have explored aspects of popular fiction. These critics have frequently defined popular art through negatives. It is not serious; it is not complicated; it is not ambiguous. Abraham Kaplan, writing in *Journal of Aesthetics,* comments that popular art is simple in the sense of being easy to understand:

> It contrasts with art in the markedly lesser demands that it makes for creative endeavor on the part of its audience. An artistic form, like a life form, is a creation, and like the living thing again, one which demands a cooperative effort, in this case between artist and audience. We cannot look to popular art for a fresh vision.[4]

Kaplan's rather caustic view of popular art focusses on the lack of aesthetic value and ignores what other critics have found to be the special value of popular art and, in particular, popular literature. That is, popular literature reflects the beliefs of the society that reads it. James D. Hart, in *The Popular Book,* comments that "In some way or another, the popular author is always the one who expresses the people's minds and paraphrases what they consider their private feelings."[5] Russel Nye has also emphasized that popular art confirms experiences rather than exploring new ones:

> For this reason, popular art has been an unusually sensitive and accurate reflector of the attitudes and concerns of the society for which it is produced. Because of its lesser quality, aesthetically, than elite art, historians and critics have tended to neglect it as a means of access to an era's—and a society's—values and ideas.[6]

It is in the reflection of the values and ideas of a society that popular literature is valuable, and the study of those beliefs contained in popular literature should deepen our understanding of the public that bought those books. While it is not safe to assume that each reader agrees with everything in the book, it does seem safe to assume that a bestseller reflects a general view of the world held by most of its readers. The formulas and conventions of popular fiction provide the keys to an understanding of the social mores of the readers.

Popular formulas have produced, for example, the western, the domestic novel and the historical romance. What these formulas have in common is the goal of escape and entertainment for the reader. They stress intensity of experience, ranging from the desperate sword fight to the agony of the heroine as she watches her fiance flirt with another woman. Through these charged incidents, the reader is momentarily freed from the drab limitations of reality. The intensity of existence, which comes to most of us in isolated moments, is multiplied and heightened in the popular novel so that within a short time the reader vicariously experiences a range of emotions that is possible to experience in no other way.

The conventions used in the formulas change as the contemporary scene changes. The blonde of the twentieth century no longer carries the same connotations as the blonde of the nineteenth century. Often though, what changes is not so much the convention as the contemporary description. For example, an extremely popular figure in nineteenth century fiction was the poor orphan. Literature now does not have many poor orphans, but it does have the young runaway. Our term for the character has changed, but he is still the young person on his own in a hostile world. Popular fiction before World War I frequently included the poor orphan, the awkward spinster, the chaste maiden, the dark brooding man, the grieving widow, the seducer, etc. Readers could be comfortable with all these characters because they were familiar and fulfilled conventional expectations.

Just as the characters in popular fiction are familiar, so too are certain events. The gunfight remains a staple of the western. The decline into alcoholism or drugs, followed by a religious conversion that saves the sinner was enormously popular in nineteenth century melodramas. The raging thunderstorm, flickering lights and strange noises have always given readers of horror stories a familiar shiver. Most familiar of all is the rescue, which is important in most popular formulas.

The study of a convention as popular as the rescue should reveal some of the basic beliefs of a society that avidly accepted the convention. John Cawelti suggests that as a culture becomes more diverse, the function of articulating and affirming cultural values, once the province of religious ritual, is taken over by the popular arts.[7]

Cawelti also acknowledges the arguments that we cannot adequately substantiate deep symbolic interpretations of a culture's inner motives and needs by examining formula fiction. Admitting the problem of an absolutely reliable analysis of the function of formulas, Cawelti says,

> I am convinced that the Freudian insight that recurrent myths and stories embody a kind of collective dreaming process is essentially correct and has an important application on the cultural as well as the universal level, that is, that the idea of a collective dream applies to formula as well as to myth.... My argument, then, is that formula stories... are structures of narrative conventions which carry out a variety of cultural functions in a unified way.[8]

The nineteenth century in America saw increasing diversity in American life. The opening of the West, the flood of immigration, the movement to the city, the surge in industrialization all created multiple societies and, therefore, multiple cultures within the expanding American society. Popular fiction provided a synthesis of these diverse values and beliefs and offered a way for millions of Americans to subscribe to uniform goals and standards. Writers found that the rescue provided a good base on which to build characters and plots that satisfied readers and reflected their values. The rescue also satisfies the essential requirement for popular work—entertainment.

The rescue is exciting. Whether the rescue comes early or late in the novel, no matter which character rescues which character, the reader gets a jolting, vicarious thrill that is much more intense than the satisfaction he gets when the heroine marries the hero or justice triumphs. William Dean Howells once wrote to Edith Wharton, "What the American public always wants is a tragedy with a happy ending."[9] The rescue convention presents potential tragedy and then averts it, thus precisely supplying what Howells said people wanted.

The rescue also embodies the American ideal of action. When Chad Buford in *The Little Shepherd of Kingdom Come* (1903) rides a desperate sixty miles to prevent Dan Dean from being shot as a guerilla, he makes a decision and acts on it.[10] The rescue is an active event, not an accident, not a fortuitous stroke of luck. The American ideal of the self-made man clearly stresses individual initiative and action. The rescue requiring decision and action fits that ideal.

Most important, the rescue is one of life's main events. It ranks with birth, death and marriage. Because of a rescue, a life may be saved, disaster averted, a dilemma solved. In popular fiction, which stresses the intensity of experience, the rescue is crucial. It involves a peak of excitement because of the very fact that it is a change in direction, a thwarting of fate, a crucial moment, a second chance, a major turning point. All the finest human qualities are involved—heroism, disregard for oneself, brotherhood, justice and (most important) the tingling acceptance of risk. There is risk in rescue for both parties, risk beyond physical danger. When events are abruptly altered, the question that arises is whether the rescue was good or bad. Should anyone try to change fate?

When the rescue is used with the romantic plot, it controls the progress and development of the romance. The convention dictates absolute standards of behavior for men and women and reinforces the accepted, traditional roles and relationships of the sexes. The convention in some instances sets the structure of the novel and in others acts as the only possible way to resolve the dilemmas of the romantic plot.

In order to examine the rescue convention, we must clearly define it. The rescue is a voluntary act on the part of the rescuer, who is neither forced to act nor paid to act. Although the idea of reward is implicit in the rescue convention, the rescuer does not act for the reward. The situations in which the rescuers act may vary to a considerable degree, and the extent of danger to the rescued party may vary, but these two limits—that the rescuer is neither forced nor paid to act—are always applicable. The elaborate escape plot is not a true rescue. In the escape situation, one character may aid another and seem to rescue, but if the second character takes a very active part in his own escape by killing guards, forcing locks, using something given to him, the situation is not a true rescue.

In the novels of the nineteenth century, there are two conventional situations where the woman is often said to have rescued the man. One is the conversion of the male to active

Christianity, away from his evil ways. Although the woman may be quite active in converting the man, there is a strong element of "Christian duty" in the situation, and we might well be dealing with another sort of convention—the conversion to Christianity.

The other conventional plot situation is that of the woman nursing the man back to health after an illness or injury. Although in the novels, the man frequently exclaims that the woman has saved his life, the situation is really part of the woman's normal duties. In domestic novels, nursing someone back to health is almost akin to running an efficient kitchen, and the situation does not fit clearly enough as an active decision on the part of the rescuer.

Another situation that is not quite a rescue is the timely confession which either frees someone or improves his status. The confession may, in fact, save someone from a terrible fate, but the act is subject to the pressures of conscience or, perhaps, the pressures of other characters. So the confessing character cannot be said to have rescued freely.

Since a rescue should be voluntary and not obligatory, the situation where an orphan is taken in by an appointed guardian is not a true rescue. The appointed guardian is not voluntary and often that very fact leads to the plot convention of the rejected orphan in a hostile home.

Series fiction using a continuing hero does not include the kind of rescues relative to this study. This kind of fiction usually spotlights a super-hero who constantly engages in daring exploits. The writer of series fiction has a definite need for continuous peaks of excitement. To examine the rescue and its implications, we must consider it in those cases where it is an option, chosen by the writer because it functioned in some particular way to support a theme or moral view.

Rescues may be divided into several types depending upon which character is rescuing and which character is being rescued. Some rescues occur simply because a character is so good that he literally rescues whenever a need arises. The heroes of both *Uncle Tom's Cabin* (1852) and *Ben-Hur* (1880) rescue members of the oppressing group when they themselves are slaves. Uncle Tom jumps into the Mississippi to rescue little Eva St. Clare; Ben-Hur saves the Roman Tribune Arrius when their ship sinks. Ishmael Worth in *Self-Raised* (1876) rescues nearly everyone in the novel, including the pasengers and crew of a sinking ocean liner.

Characters frequently prove their nobility by rescuing enemies or rivals in love. Horatio Alger's hero Grant Colburn (*Digging for Gold, a Story of California,* 1891) rescues the villain Dionysius Silverthorn from Indians; Gertrude in *The Lamplighter* (1854) saves Isabel from drowning even though Isabel appears to have won the love of Gertrude's sweetheart.

The types of rescues strongly connected with romance in popular novels before 1916, however, are the rescue of a child, the rescue from physical danger of a female by a male, the rescue from a dilemma of a female by a male, and the rescue of a male by a female. These four support and, in fact, dictate the structure of the romantic story in the novels as well as define acceptable male and female roles.

The rescue of a child was an extremely popular convention in the domestic novel, but it also was used in novels of adventure. It appears with fair regularity throughout the period from 1800 to 1916. It was apparently so popular that novelists writing books about social issues often used part of the pattern to catch the reader's attention. The rescue of a child established the structure of the romantic plot in the novel. It also provided the opportunity for the rescued child to develop the acceptable standards and values of society and grow up to be a respectable and successful adult.

The rescue from physical danger of a female by a male is unquestionably the most popular rescue pattern. The form of the rescue does not alter much over the years. Women scream and men save them. The later novels, however, sometimes present a broader situation, allowing the male to rescue someone close to the female and obtain the same results as if the female were rescued. The structure of this rescue and the fact that it changes so little offers an interesting area for exploration of the American view of male and female roles.

Appearing in fiction after the Civil War is the male rescue of a female from a dilemma. The dilemma is used primarily in the domestic novel, and its position in the structure of the plot differs from the position of the physical rescue. The dilemma rescue also differs from the physical rescue in the kind of man doing the rescuing, in what is being proved, and in the emphasis in the results of the rescue. The dilemma rescue, like the physical rescue, reflects society's views of male and female roles, and also apparently reflects the changing position of women after the Civil War.

The fourth romantic rescue is the rescue of a man by a woman. This act is the least consistent of the four, but it may well be the most interesting. The rescue by a female divides into two patterns, depending upon whether the woman is white or Indian. The Indian woman rescues quite efficiently and quite consistently. The white woman rescues in a variety of situations which do not form a clear pattern. Often she rescues in a far less dangerous situation than the Indian, and there are strangely mixed results. The fact that writers who used formulas consistently had difficulty using the rescue convention as it applied to females rescuing males rather clearly reflects the idea that women rescuing men was considered unnatural. Women were expected to nurse men back to health or convert them to the true faith, but beyond these clearly defined situations, the rules were murky.

Beginning with the earliest novels, popular writers claimed a moral or didactic purpose for their work. The introduction to *Malaeska; The Indian Wife of the White Hunter* (1860), the first dime novel, contains the following:

> It is chosen as the initial volume of the Dime Novel series, from the chaste characters of its delineations, from the interest which attaches to its fine picture of border life and Indian adventure, and from the real romance of its incidents. It is American in all its features, pure in its tone, elevating in its sentiments.... it is hoped to reach all... to instill a pure and elevating sentiment in the hearts and minds of the people.[11]

This lofty description of purpose is typical of that usually given for popular fiction. In fact, of course, the novels were written and published to make money. And at the same time, the readers were not reading for edification. They read for entertainment. They read, as Kaplan emphasizes, to see a world "not as it is, nor even as it might be, but as we would have it."[12] The rescue convention in the romantic plots shows us what kind of romantic world those readers wanted to have.

Chapter II

The Rescue of a Child

The appealing child in want or in danger has always represented a guaranteed means of getting a sentimental reaction from any audience. Therefore it is not surprising that writers of popular novels frequently used the convention of the rescue of a child. Since the convention usually was placed at the beginning of the novel, readers were caught immediately by the pathetic situation of a helpless child in trouble.

In its most conventional form, the rescue of a child controls the course of the novel. For the purposes of this study, we will consider a child as age fifteen or under. At age fifteen, the relative helplessness of an individual becomes less clear since in the nineteenth century it was possible for boys to earn a living and for girls to marry at that age. The rescue situation opens the novel as the child (almost always an orphan) is found in a serious danger or dilemma. The danger may be imminent death, or a cruel stepparent/aunt/guardian, or the total absence of a guiding and protective adult. Since the child is not old enough to function independently in an adult world, the rescue is crucial, in an immediate sense, in providing care and support and, in the future sense, in allowing the child to grow into a productive person.

The rescue moves the child from the immediate danger and from whatever social environment he is in. The new environment is often, but not always, in a better social class. However, the new situation always offers safety and an opportunity to reach adulthood.

In its full pattern the rescue, by putting the child into a new atmosphere, also puts him in immediate contact with his future loved one. Frequently, the future romance is signaled to the reader by the immediate affection the two children develop for each other. Readers knowing the pattern, as most of them surely did, could be confident that the novel would provide a satisfactory romantic situation.

The rescued child is going to be the main character of the

novel, and usually most of the novel concerns his adult life, its trials and tribulations, and, of course, romance. The rescue situation in the opening generates the reader's immediate concern in the welfare of the child. Once this concern is established, the reader will naturally wish to continue learning about the adventures of the hero or heroine.

The usual pattern for the rescue of a child, then, is to provide instant sentimental appeal as the novel opens by showing a helpless child in difficulty. The rescue itself moves the child to a significantly improved social environment and puts him in contact with his future loved one. Once the child is established as the main character, the novel concentrates on his adult life. The last major element in the pattern is that eventually the child pays back the debt incurred by his rescue. The repayment may take a variety of forms, but it is always an affirmation of the rightness of the rescue of this child so many pages back.

Augusta Evans Wilson's novel *Beulah* (1859) illustrates the full pattern of the convention of the rescue of a child. The novel opens with thirteen-year-old Beulah Benton and her younger sister, Lilly, in an orphanage. Since Lilly is the pretty one, she is adopted. Beulah is sent out as a nursemaid to a family interested in cheap labor. Things get worse for Beulah. The couple that adopted Lilly refuses to let Beulah see her sister, who dies shortly thereafter of scarlet fever. Beulah is now alone, friendless, and in a situation that would condemn her to a life of menial labor.

At this crucial point in the story, Dr. Guy Hartwell sees poor Beulah's tear-streaked, homely little face bending over her sister's coffin. (Wilson spends a great deal of time telling us how homely Beulah is, probably to emphasize how altruistic the coming rescue must be.) Dr. Hartwell, although he has been introduced as a cold, unfriendly man, is quick to offer refuge. "Beulah, come home with me. Be my child; my daughter."[1] Beulah rejects rescue. "No. You too would hate me for my ugliness. Let me hide it in the grave with Lilly. They cannot separate us there" (p. 44). Dr. Hartwell, a man not used to being refused, takes more positive action by lifting her into his carriage and taking her to his spacious mansion. "I am glad I have you safe under my own roof, where no more cruel injustice can assail you" (p. 45). Beulah has been rescued. She is given an education and all the material advantages.

She does, however, refuse to be adopted formally and continually remarks upon the debt she owes to Hartwell. Completing her education, she gets a teaching job. This independent action upsets Hartwell, who wants her to live an idle life. "Relinquish the idea of teaching. Let me present you to society as my adopted child. Thus you can requite the debt" (p. 148). Children are not rescued in popular fiction to live idle lives, however, and Beulah refuses his request. "God knows I am grateful.... Oh, that it were in my power to prove to you my gratitude" (p. 148). The obligation of the child to repay his rescue is very strong in the convention, but few novels discuss the necessary payment as endlessly as *Beulah* does.

The bulk of the novel is concerned with Beulah's adult life. Very independent, she goes from teaching to writing and becomes moderately successful. This career development is amid a stream of domestic complications, insults from society about her humble origin, and romantic crises involving Beulah and a wide circle of friends.

Finally, however, the rescue must be repaid. Hartwell comes to see Beulah where she is living in the modest cottage that she has paid for with her earnings from writing. He proposes marriage, but Beulah refuses. After four more years of career and domestic crises, however, she realizes where her heart is. When Hartwell proposes again, she accepts. Now, after all the talk of the debt, Hartwell wants to be loved for himself. "Beulah, do you cling to me because you love me? or because you pity me? or because you are grateful to me for past love and kindness?" (p. 432). "Because you are my all," she answers. Beulah repays her rescuer by making him happy in marriage. Furthermore, her rescue when she was a child did put her in immediate contact with the future loved one, just as the pattern dictates.

Beulah was very successful, selling 30,000 copies within four years.[2] Wilson knew enough to keep a good pattern going and used the rescue of a child for her next book, *St. Elmo* (1867), one of the all-time best sellers in American fiction. Her heroine in this book is Edna Earl, who achieves greater personal success than Beulah did, has a stronger interest in religion, and is prettier. These are the only major differences between the books as Wilson once more used the rescue of a child to structure the novel.

In *St. Elmo* twelve-year-old Edna Earl (an orphan) lives with her grandfather and his second wife. Within a few pages, both old people die, and Edna is left alone. She sets out for Columbus, Georgia, where she has heard that children can get work in factories. There is a train wreck:

> She was held fast between timbers, one of which seemed to have fallen across her feet and crushed them, as she was unable to move them, and was conscious of a horrible sensation of numbness; one arm, too, was pinioned at her side."[3]

Edna sustains a broken foot and dislocated shoulder. Her pet dog is killed in the wreck, leaving her completely alone and friendless. At this low point in her life, the widow Mrs. Murray comes along and takes her in:

> "What splendid eyes she has! Poor little thing! Of course you will come and prescribe for her, and I will see that she is carefully nursed until she is quite well again" (p. 33).

Edna is so charming that Mrs. Murray makes the arrangement permanent, and Edna is rescued from an uncertain fate:

> "Child, will you trust your future and your education to me? I do not mean that I will teach you—oh! no—but I will have you thoroughly educated, so that when you are grown you can support yourself by teaching. I have no daughter.... I shall prove a good friend and protector till you are eighteen, and capable of providing for yourself" (p. 38).

Edna has been taken from friendless poverty to the estate of a wealthy woman. Her environment has clearly improved.

Following the pattern, Edna shortly meets Mrs. Murray's son, St. Elmo, who is the dark, brooding, dangerous hero so popular in fiction:

> ...the fair, chiseled lineaments were blotted by dissipation, and blackened and distorted by the baleful fires of a fierce, passionate nature, and a restless, powerful, and unhallowed intellect...the ungovernable flames of sin had reduced him... (p. 40).

Just the sort of man to be reformed by love! But first Edna has to grow up. She studies diligently and becomes a religious scholar and world famous author, turning down proposals from virtually every male in the book. She prays continually for St. Elmo, until he at last leaves his life of total dissipation and becomes a minister. "Can you be a minister's wife, and aid him as only you can? Oh, my darling, my darling! I never expect to be worthy of you. But you can make me less unworthy" (p. 486). In reforming and then marrying St.Elmo, Edna thoroughly repays Mrs. Murray's rescue of her from that train wreck.

The novel that excited Hawthorne's frustration, Maria Cummins' *The Lamplighter* (1854), also was structured around the rescue of a child. The novel begins by introducing the ragged and unloved eight-year-old orphan Gertrude. Gertrude, whose only joy is her pet kitten, lives with a woman who beats her and becomes enraged when she discovers the kitten:

> Gerty heard a sudden splash and a piercing cry. Nan had flung the poor creature into a large vessel of steaming hot water.... The little animal struggled and writhed an instant, then died in torture.[4]

Gertrude throws a stick at Nan and, in turn, is thrown out of the house to wander the streets alone. Fortunately, she is rescued.

The kindly lamplighter, Trueman Flint, takes her into his home. Gertrude's original social level was so low that even a humble lamplighter's home is an elevation of status. Her new home is also far superior to the old one in warmth and happiness. Young Willie Sullivan lives in the same building, so Gertrude meets her future love very quickly.

Gertrude grows into a fine young woman. However, the lamplighter dies by the time she is grown, and she cannot truly repay the rescue to him in an active way although she has made his life very happy. She also rescues someone else later in the novel, thus affirming the importance of her own rescue. In many novels, bringing happiness and contentment to the rescuer's life is an important part of the repayment made by the child.

An earlier example of the rescue of a child in American popular fiction occurs in Jessee Holman's *The Prisoners of Niagara or Errors of Education* (1810). This novel opens with the hero, a colonial rebel, held prisoner in a British fort. But Holman quickly flashes back to show the hero at eighteen months being stolen from his Indian captors by William Evermont, a trapper. Since in popular fiction anything is better than being held by Indians, young William (named after his rescuer) has been rescued from a terrible fate and transferred to a better environment. The trapper deposits the child with a farm family and moves on. Unfortunately, the family turns out to be cruel to the child, and by age five he needs another rescue. Playing in the woods with his puppy, he sees a well-dressed gentleman ride by. Getting directly to the point, Williams says to the man, "I want a better father. Will you be my father?"[5] The gentleman agrees "with the fondest look" our hero has ever seen (p. 46). The gentleman promises to come back in the morning and get him. This rescue occurs none too soon since that night William's puppy is killed by the nasty boy in his adopted family, and William runs away.

Holman rushes along the rest of the pattern by having a five-year-old William jump into the Potomac the next morning and rescue two-year-old Zerelda Engleton:

> Young as I was, the hope of assisting a suffering being, overcome [sic] the idea of danger so natural to the infant mind, and I flew in an instant to the place from whence the noise preceded (p. 48).

Zerelda, it turns out, is the niece of Major Hayland, who (not very surprisingly) is the gentleman who had said he would be William's father. So, William repays his own rescue immediately and comes in contact with his future loved one. His social class is markedly improved—he is now in the American class of landed gentry who mingle with British aristocracy. The rest of the novel catalogues his growing up, his education, and his sexual and military adventures. In the end, he marries Zerelda after Holman has used another rescue convention, the rescue from physical danger of a female by a male, to settle the romance.

Although the whole pattern of the rescue of a child is present in this early novel, it is not as clearly or successfully controlled as in the mid-century novels of Wilson and Cummins. Holman has to have his child rescued twice. An eighteen-month-old baby might need rescuing, but he does not have the endearing personality that a five-year-old can have. The first rescue, therefore, is wasted effort in terms of effectively snaring the reader's sentimental interest when measured next to the second rescue.

The second major structural problem Holman has is in putting the repayment of the rescue immediately after the rescue itself. The repayment placed at the end of a novel gives a finished look to the plot, a rounding off of events, and it affirms the innate worth of the hero and the original rescue. Wilson and Cummins both build to the repayment situation while Holman wastes its dramatic and conclusive effect by putting it in the beginning of the novel.

Another novelist in the first half of the nineteenth century made ineffective use of the convention in his novel *Wyoming, a Tale* (1845). Caleb Wright tells a story of pioneers in northern Pennsylvania. In a brief flashback, he reveals that Colonel Dinning's daughter, Ruth, was adopted by the childless colonel when an old Indian woman literally left the three-year-old girl on the doorstep.[6] The colonel is wealthy, and, again, anything is better than living with the Indians, so Ruth is certainly rescued. Wright, however, wastes the possible interest generated by such an episode when he simply has one of the characters relate the story. He also fails to introduce Ruth's future love until she is ten years old—the kind of gap most novelists using the convention did not allow. Moreover, Ruth is not the main character of the book. She is not, in fact, very important except that she eventually marries the hero. She never does anything specific to repay her rescue, except that she brings a good deal of happiness to the colonel.

From these early weak uses of the convention, we can see that the domestic novelists of the mid-century probably were responsible for developing the rescue of a child so that it controlled the movement of a novel. Once this pattern was established in a successful way, the rescue of a child was used over and over by popular novelists.

It was used even by a writer like Hamlin Garland whose reputation rests on his realistic portrayal of Midwestern frontier farm life. Garland's *A Little Norsk or Ol' Pap's Flaxen* (1892) is built on the rescue of a child. On a cold winter day on the plains of Dakota territory, partners Anson Wood and Bert Gearheart take in a five-year-old orphan from a neighboring farm. Her father has been lost in a blizzard, and her mother has frozen to death in their cabin.[7] Obviously, little Flaxen is in a dangerous situation, and when the two partners take her in, she is moved to a place of safety. There is no rise in social level as in the earlier novels. Since no one claims her, Flaxen grows up with the two men, goes to school, and at the age of fifteen marries a young man from a nearby town. She has repaid Anson by filling his life with the happiness of fatherhood and then grandfatherhood. After Flaxen marries, Bert realizes that he has fallen in love with her, and he goes west to forget her.

Her husband turns out to be a scoundrel and a thief. Fortunately, he is soon killed in an accident. Flaxen and Anson live quite happily for a time. Then Bert returns. He asks Anson, "Say, it seems pretty well understood that you're her father— but where do I come in?" (p. 156). Anson tells him that he "ought to be her husband," and everything is settled, apparently to the satisfaction of all parties. Both men have been repaid for their original rescue of Flaxen. This slight novel by Garland is structured almost entirely around the pattern of the rescue of a child. Aside from some realistic details of daily life, the novel contains only the plot elements comprising the convention.

Another rescue of a child in Dakota territory takes place in William Lillibridge's *Ben Blair, The Story of a Plainsman* (1905). Eight-year-old Ben Blair watches his drunken father set fire to the house in which Ben's mother has just died. While the fire rages, Ben huddles under the house, hoping the flames won't reach him. After the flames subside, Ben crawls out and looks at "the charred, unrecognizable corpse of his mother."[8] Wealthy rancher Rankin comes along after seeing the flames from his ranch and helps Ben bury his mother. Then Rankin takes him home and raises him. In true laconic western style, Rankin answers a brief "yes" when Ben asks him, "Am I to—to stay with you?" (p. 42). Ben is now living on a prosperous ranch and is under the guidance of a man who can properly serve as a model for manhood. Within two days of his rescue, Ben visits a neighboring ranch and meets five-year-old Florence Baker, his future love.

Ben's repayment of his rescue is in the western tradition. He hunts down and captures Rankin's killer—Ben's father who has reappeared after all these years. Ben then has to defend Tom Blair from an angry lynch mob in town. His repayment continues when he discovers papers in Rankin's safe which clearly indicate that Rankin was really Ben's father. Because Rankin obviously did not want the facts known while he lived, Ben decides to preserve his secret. He destroys the papers and decides never to tell anyone. This repayment of the original rescue follows the code of honor stressed in the western formula. Ben keeps his rescuer's secret, hunts down his killer, and then defends the killer from a lynch mob, supporting the code of justice Rankin had taught him. He wins his love, Florence, on the last page of the novel.

In contrast to the western novel of action, a bestseller that has almost no action and is concerned almost entirely with a portrayal of the homely virtues is Irving Bacheller's *Eben Holden* (1900), which sold 250,000 copies.[9] The title character is the rescuer here. The story opens with Eben carrying six-year-old Willie on his back in a basket. Willie's entire family drowned while on a picnic, and Eben, a penniless farmhand, takes the boy away rather than letting him be sent to the county home. Willie feels "very warm and cozy wrapped in the big shawl."[10] Here the improvement in environment is in the fact that Eben offers personal attention and caring in contrast to the impersonal county home. Bacheller, in fact, has lowered Willie's social level by moving him from the position of a son of a prosperous farmer to the companion of an itinerant farm worker. But this variation in the general pattern is clearly connected to Bacheller's purpose in the novel of presenting the virtues inherent in the New England rural people.

Eben takes work at the farm of David Brower where Willie meets Hope Brower, "a barefooted little girl a bit older than I, with red cheeks and blue eyes and long curly hair, that shone like gold in the sunlight" (p. 70). Bacheller is less concerned than some other writers with the repayment element of the convention. Because Bacheller is emphasizing goodness as a way of life and as its own reward, Willie repays his rescue by growing up to be a good and successful man. In the world of this novel, such a development is ample repayment.

An equally successful regional novel is John Fox, Jr.'s *The Little Shepherd of Kingdom Come* (1903), set in Kentucky. This novel has sold over a million and a quarter copies over the years, and thirty years after publication was one of the books in highest demand in libraries.[11] Like Jessee Holman in 1810, Fox has his child rescued twice. But unlike Holman, Fox employs one of the most highly developed rescue plots to control the structure of his novel. Both of the rescues are connected to later events, and they are also connected to other types of rescues.

The novel opens with the young orphan Chad wandering the mountains of Kentucky with his dog. The Turner family takes him in, in the casual way of the mountain people by giving him supper and a bed and then just expecting him to stay. In spite of the casual attitude of the family, Chad definitely is being rescued. In this mountain society, such a rescue is natural. "Already the house was full of children and dependents, but no word passed between old Joel and the old mother, for no word was necessary" (p. 27). Although Chad is not surrounded with wealth, he is surrounded with a large, caring family. He also meets Melissa Turner with tangled yellow hair and large, solemn eyes. Melissa is also adopted. She will be prominent later in the novel as a female rescuing a male.

Chad lives happily in the mountains for a year. On a visit to Lexington, he hurts his foot, gets left behind by his party, and becomes lost and hungry. Major Calvin Buford passes by in his carriage. And the second rescue is underway. Chad gets a ride, a meal and goes to a horse auction with the Major. By the end of the day, Major Buford takes him home and asks him, "Wouldn't you like to stay here in the Bluegrass now and go to school?" (p. 90). Chad says he thinks he probably would and everything is settled. By this rescue Chad is elevated to living in a fine town house with the leading citizen of Lexington. His life now promises education, culture and opportunity. The Major's neighbor is General Dean, who has a daughter, Margaret, a little girl with "dancing black eyes" (p. 98). Chad has been in his new home only one day when he meets the girl he is to love. Margaret will figure later in the novel in the rescue of a female by a male.

Having carefully constructed two totally satisfactory rescues for his child, Fox moves the action of the novel back and forth between the mountains and the town. Chad grows up well educated, honest, thoughtful and courageous. But he joins the Union side in the Civil War and thereby wounds both the Turner family and Major Buford, all of whom are loyal to the South. This division of families in the war is one of Fox's major themes. There is no question that Chad is a fine adult, but he cannot truly repay his rescues because of his betrayal of the rescuer's political beliefs. Bitter feeling results as he goes to war. When the war is over, Margaret tells him that the major forgave him before he died. On a visit back to the hills, Chad sees Mother Turner, who "broke down and threw her arms around him and cried" (p. 313). It is because of the impossibility of repaying those childhood rescues and particularly the impossibility of repaying Melissa, who has rescued him, that Chad does not allow himself to accept the offered happiness with Margaret at the end of the novel. He heads west "starting his life ever afresh, with his old capital, a strong body and a stout heart" (p. 336).

Fox's balancing of three rescue conventions in the novel testifies to his control over the patterns. His two rescues of Chad reflect the two essential ways to improve a child's environment. The rescue by Major Buford brings Chad the opportunity for wealth and education. The rescue by the Turner family gives Chad a loving, supportive home.

Fox's sophisticated balancing of rescue patterns did not necessarily reflect a major shift in popular fiction. The original standard pattern continued to sell. Jean Webster's *Daddy-Long-Legs* (1912) introduces seventeen-year-old Jerusha Abbott, the oldest orphan in the orphanage. Jerusha is plucked from the orphanage and sent off to college by an anonymous trustee of the orphanage who is described as cold and odd.[12] The only condition of the college education as explained by the matron is that Jerusha must write to the trustee every month and report her progress:

> "That is—you are not to thank him for the money; he doesn't care to have that mentioned, but you are to write a letter telling of your progress in your studies and the details of your daily life" (p. 14).

Mrs. Lippert stresses that these letters are the only payment required.

Jerusha writes faithfully while she completes her education, and she continues to write to her benefactor when she becomes a successful author. She wins a scholarship and can support herself. Finally, she sells her novel and becomes successful. The benefactor at last reveals that he is Jervis Pendleton, whom she has known as a friend's uncle. Jervis proposes. "We belong to each other now," she writes to him in her final letter (p. 303). And so Jerusha repays her rescuer by marrying him and making him happy. If all this sounds quite familiar, it is because Webster's novel has much the same plot as *Beulah*, and, although Jerusha at seventeen is older than the other orphans, she is included here to show how Wilson's rescue pattern and plot can reappear nearly sixty years later and be as successful as ever.

Although the domestic novelists used the rescue of a child more often than other writers did, novelists concerned with social issues sometimes used the convention to open their novels. Again, because the rescue so effectively captured the initial interest of the readers, it assured the writer an audience for his social views.

In 1875 Josiah Holland wrote a muckraking novel about the immoral business practices in New England mill towns. He begins the novel, *Sevenoaks: a Story of Today*, by introducing mill owner Robert Belcher, who has cheated and driven inventor Paul Benedict insane. Benedict is in the poorhouse with his small son Harry. Jim Fenton, a trapper and old friend of Benedict's, comes to town and sees the boy weeping. "He was thinly and very shabbily clad, and was shivering with cold. The great, healthy heart within Jim Fenton was touched in an instant."[13]

Holland varies the rescue pattern in that Fenton also has to rescue Harry's insane father from the poorhouse. They all go to live in the woods. Harry is not the main character of the novel and does not grow up in the book. Therefore, there is no need for a little girl to appear, and the full rescue pattern does not appear. But Harry does repay his rescue by recalling his father from insanity through prayer. When Jim Fenton fails to cure his friend with good food and clean air, he tells Harry that the boy's father is not getting better and Harry must pray.

> The boy was serious.... He had said his prayers many times when he did not know that he wanted anything. Here was a great emergency.... He... was the only one who could pray for the life of his father (p. 91).

After some concentrated effort by Harry, his father suddenly has a look "full of intelligence and peace" (p. 92). The little boy through prayer has "fetched 'im" as Jim says (p. 93).

Another novel concerned with business ethics was the enormously popular *The Winning of Barbara Worth* (Harold Bell Wright, 1911). The book sold 1,635,000 copies by 1941.[14] Wright used two rescues of children to start his novel. The main rescue is clearly inserted only for initial interest. Jefferson Worth, a Colorado banker, and his party are traveling through the Mojave Desert when they find an abandoned wagon. Up ahead lies a dead woman. A four-year-old girl is toddling around the body, wailing, "Barba wants a drink."[15] "Jefferson Worth reached her first" (p. 43). Barbara has been rescued. She grows up to be a lovely young woman amid many advantages. Although she is the title character, she is not really the main focus of the novel which is concerned with political and financial machinations in the development of Colorado mines and towns. No other part of the rescue pattern is used. In the structure of the novel, Wright has no clear need for this rescue.

The second rescue of a child took place before the novel begins, but we learn while the men ride through the desert that ten-year-old Abe Lee (in Worth's party) was left an orphan in a mining camp and was taken up by an engineer known as the Seer. "He has been with me ever since," comments the Seer (p. 28). Again, the rest of the pattern is missing. Abe does become a valuable engineer and is a trusted employee of Jefferson Worth; but since Worth did not rescue him, it cannot be said that Abe ever repays his rescue as the pattern would dictate. Since Wright's novel is actually an investigation of business ethics, it seems clear that he is only using the rescue convention to get the novel going, and he must have felt such a start was important since there are two rescues of children in the opening pages.

The consistently bestselling author Gertrude Atherton used the child rescue to open her novel *Patience Sparhawk and Her Times* (1895).[16] Fifteen-year-old Patience is left an orphan when her drunken mother dies in a fire. Patience is taken in by Mr. Foord, an elderly gentleman of reduced fortune but much refinement. Because of his age, Mr. Foord sends Patience off to his half-sister Miss Tremont in San Francisco. Patience's social level has been raised and improved. Her moral surroundings are now beyond reproach. (Miss Tremont is a temperance leader.) Her educational opportunities are numerous. Atherton's primary theme in the novel is woman's independent spirit and the degree to which she can properly exercise that spirit. Although Atherton used the rescue of a child to begin the novel, she did not allow the convention to control the ending of the book. She did, however, use another rescue pattern, the male rescuing the female from a dilemma, to end the novel. That novelists who were interested in social issues used even part of the convention demonstrates the appeal of the convention to readers.

Structurally, in the novels which used the whole pattern, the writer had a convention that gave a framework to whatever story he wished to tell. The rescue of a child opened the novel at a fast pace and held the reader's natural interest in the fate of a charming youngster. Since the child was moved to an improved environment, often a better social class, the writer was free to work out subsequent events in a setting more attractive than the original depressing surroundings. Most bestselling popular novelists avoided extensive discussion of social problems and since they wished to end the books happily, they needed to place the main characters in promising circumstances.

The rescue pattern, after moving the child to a better situation, puts him in immediate contact with the future sweetheart. The writer can begin the romantic plot at once—a plot that the readers confidently expected all domestic novels at least to provide. The romance was never settled until the end of the novel, so the writer using the rescue pattern had a book-length thread of interest in which to tangle other plot complications. The repayment part of the pattern was important to the novel's structure in that it rewarded the rescuer, affirmed the validity of the novel's opening event, brought the novel full circle, and finished off the original episode.

The rescue makes it possible for these children to become adults. What kind of adults are they? The qualities they display as adults can tell us something about the social and moral values of the readers. From a humanitarian standpoint, all children are worth rescuing. However, the rescued children in the novels usually make a definite contribution to society, further proving the importance of their rescues. Because these novels were so popular, we must conclude that the qualities the children have as adults were considered desirable by a majority of readers.

All the children grow up to be moral, upright citizens. The chance to lead a good, honest life was the primary opportunity resulting from the rescue. Only two children, however, offered nothing more to society than good lives. In *Wyoming, a Tale*, Ruth Dinning grows up to be a charming young lady and finally marries the hero. And Harold Bell Wright's heroine Barbara Worth develops into a vibrant, beautiful young woman, who charms every male in the novel. It is probably significant that both writers here are male, and the children in the books are female. As we will see, these writers do not allow the male children rescued in their novels to lead merely good lives. But even as late as 1911, it was enough that a young lady be charming.

There was another way for young ladies to serve society— three of them married the men who took them from poverty. When Beulah agrees to marry Dr. Hartwell, he sighs, "At last, then, after years of sorrow, and pain, and bitterness, I shall be happy in my own home; shall have a wife, a companion, who loves me for myself alone" (p. 433). Beulah's material success is important as a contribution to society, but when she brings comfort to this lonely man that, too, is an important contribution. And until Flaxen in Garland's novel is ready to marry Bert, he wanders through the West, accomplishing nothing, amounting to nothing, accumulating nothing. With Flaxen as his wife, Bert is going to settle down and run a dray with his old partner Anson. The marriage to Flaxen will vastly improve his life. Another orphan turned writer, Jerusha in *Daddy-Long-Legs*, marries her benefactor and brightens his solitary, though wealthy, life. Her last letter says they are "both very, very happy" (p. 303).

The men are lonely—they need good women. Women can make a clearcut contribution by bringing both happiness and direction to men's lives. These three novels are dated 1859, 1892 and 1912 respectively. Obviously, this social value lasted through the years. It is also significant that these are all May-December unions. (Wilson, in fact, specialized in romances with substantial age gaps between the men and women. Beulah is seventeen years younger than Dr. Hartwell, and Edna Earl is twenty-two years younger than St. Elmo.) There is no doubt in the novels about whether such matches are wise. In the world of the novels, such matches were very sensible.

The most consistent virtue expressed in the adult lives of these rescued children is that of becoming a hard-working, productive member of society. None of the characters grows up to be a criminal or vagrant. Not all, of course, were able to equal the achievements of Edna Earl (*St. Elmo*). She becomes an international religious scholar, widely respected and sought after. She literally wears down her health in trying to satisfy her eager public. Wilson's other heroine, Beulah, also becomes a famous writer, as does Jerusha in *Daddy-Long-Legs*. Gertrude Atherton has her independent heroine, Patience Sparhawk, become a successful writer. It is probably not surprising that the novelists chose writing as the professions of their heroines, but all the writers also stress how hard the women work and how successful they become. Until marriage takes them to another area of endeavor and a different kind of social service, the women work very hard in one of the few work situations open to the middle-class woman in the nineteenth century. The female writers, unlike the male writers, made certain that their heroines actively contributed to society before they went on to support the family structure by marrying.

Bacheller's child hero Willie (*Eben Holden*) grows up to be a writer for the New York *Tribune*. After being wounded in the Spanish-American War, Willie goes into politics. Since the basis of this novel is the depiction of good people leading good lives, Willie will contribute to society by bringing morality to politics. Serving in the war shows that he is a man who does his duty.

Although Harold Bell Wright allows Barbara Worth to grow up and contribute nothing but charm to the world, he does not allow the rescued boy in his novel to do so little. Without any formal training, Abe Lee becomes an engineer, and he is the standard in the novel against which Easterners are measured. Abe Lee can do almost anything. He figures out where to place irrigation channels, something the developers and pioneers desperately need. Later, he rescues valuable property and averts tragedy. When an Eastern engineer questions Lee's lack of formal training, banker Jefferson Worth snaps, "We have only one standard in the West, Mr.

Holmes. What can you do?" (p. 113).

As another kind of service, mid-century novels often used spiritual reform or guidance as the contribution by the rescued child. When *St. Elmo* begins, Edna Earl clearly has her work of redemption cut out for her. Since she develops into a religious scholar, she not only prays for the dark, tormented St. Elmo but also has long conversations with him about the Greek idea of self-improvement, the Coptic civilization, and the doctrines of Zoroaster. At last St. Elmo is redeemed from his life of depravity. "My precious Edna, no oath shall ever soil my lips again.... I loath my past life.... My Edna—my own wife, shall save me!" (p. 283). It is not until St. Elmo actually becomes a minister that Edna feels her work is complete, and she agrees to marry him. By saving St. Elmo from dissipation, Edna, of course, has saved a soul—always a worthy endeavor. Converting men from the evil ways was a common role for fictional heroines.

It might seem obvious that in a convention dealing with rescues, one way of becoming valuable to society is by more rescues. Jessee Holman in *The Prisoners of Niagara, or Errors of Education* has five-year-old William Evermont jump into the Potomac to rescue Zerelda Engleton. This rescue not only repays his own rescue but also establishes his courage. Many of the children demonstrate both moral and physical courage when they grow up.

Gertrude in *The Lamplighter* rescues her supposed rival in love. While at Saratoga, Gertrude has encountered her childhood sweetheart, Willie Sullivan. Not only has Willie apparently forgotten her, he is being very attentive to Isabel Clinton, a well-known flirt. Gertrude, of course, is crushed. "She wept as the broken-hearted weep" (p. 262). A few days later, the steamboat on which Gertrude is returning to New York City catches fire. Gertrude finds herself clinging to the same rope as Isabel Clinton. Another passenger comes to Gertrude's aid. She decides to save Isabel rather than herself because "Willie would weep for her loss, and that must not be" (p. 297). Isabel is rescued, and, fortunately, Gertrude is also picked up by a later rescue boat. At the end of the novel, Gertrude learns that her sacrifice would have been for nothing since Willie does indeed still love her. Her noble gesture, however, clearly shows a courage and greatness of spirit, virtues that are invaluable to society. Chad Buford in *The Little Shepherd of Kingdom Come* rides sixty miles to save a childhood friend from being shot by Yankees. The ride is not only physically dangerous; but it demonstrates Chad's fine character since he is on the Union side, and the novel deals with divided loyalties. These particular rescues, then, emphasize personal courage and the concern for others that transcends selfishness.

Some of the children grow up and perform acts which reflect clear ideas of social justice, giving immediate benefits to society. Little Harry (*Sevenoaks; a Story of Today*) not only saves his father through prayer but he is instrumental in the final ruin of the villain Belcher and in the restoration of his father's business rights. Harry's youthful innocence influences Mrs. Dillingham, who exposes Belcher's shady financial records, subsequently ruining him. The rescue of a child here supports Holland's social purpose in writing. Holland's child needs rescuing because of the business corruption the novel says is pervasive in American life, and the child helps end that corruption at the end of the book. Also supporting justice, Abe Lee (*The Winning of Barbara Worth*) makes a spectacular ride to bring the payroll to the miners after the bank, controlled by corrupt interests, refuses to release the money. And Ben Blair, though wounded, holds off a lynch mob successfully, and so upholds law and order.

All these values—becoming upright citizens, being good wives, being hard working and productive, offering spiritual help, displaying physical and ethical courage, contributing to social justice—provide definite benefits to society. Readers continued to buy books that expressed such ideas, showing their support and acceptance of those values.

A primary social belief implicit in the rescue of a child is the idea that environment is the factor that determines one's development. The rescued children come from a variety of backgrounds. Barbara Worth is a nameless waif wandering in the desert; Flaxen is the daughter of Norwegian pioneers; little Willie (*Eben Holden*) is the son of a rich farmer. The backgrounds, however, are not as important as the environments to which the children are moved. Each new environment offers not only personal safety, but also an opportunity for the child to develop whatever talents he may possess. Central to this development is education.

Education has an unquestioned value in the system of social beliefs revealed in these novels. In some cases, the rescue is based on an offer of education. Jerusha Abbott (*Daddy-Long-Legs*) is offered a college education by a trustee of the orphanage. The terms of her rescue are precisely stated as tuition, board, books, and $35 a month allowance. Jerusha is not in any physical danger but she is facing a life of drudgery. Her rescue consists entirely of the opportunity for an education, the only thing she needs to develop her writing talents. During her sophomore year in college, Jerusha wins a short story contest and is on her way to success.

In Fox's *The Little Shepherd of Kingdom Come*, Major Buford specifically asks Chad if he wants to go to school. "Chad's eyes lighted up. 'I reckon I would' " (p. 90). Augusta Evans Wilson includes education as an important element in the rescues in both her novels. Edna Earl is offered an education by Mrs. Murray so that she can become a teacher. And Dr. Hartwell offers Beulah Benton an education when he takes her home to his mansion. In spite of the insults she endures from Hartwell's sister, Beulah clings to her educational opportunity as the way to become self-supporting and make something of herself.

Even when education is not mentioned at the moment of rescue, the child usually is given an opportunity for schooling in his new environment. Barbara Worth is educated to be a refined, cultured young lady, the proper daughter of a banker. Ben Blair is educated to handle the business of running a ranch. William Evermont (*The Prisoners of Niagara, or Errors of Education*) does brilliantly in school. Even the two pioneer bachelors raising Flaxen believe in the value of education. She is sent to a city school when she is fourteen even though the men will be lonely without her. Willie in *Eben Holden* goes to school in town and then goes on to college. Patience Sparhawk has always been an avid reader. When she goes to San Francisco, she gets a good education. Gertrude in *The Lamplighter* is educated when she goes to live with rich Miss Graham after the lamplighter's death. In all the cases, a good education is the crucial factor in the child's development.

So important was education considered in the future prospects of a child that Holland's novel introduces this value even though Harry does not grow up in the book. Harry Benedict is living happily with his father and his rescuer Jim Fenton in the woods. The healthful atmosphere of the outdoors is superior to the corrupt atmosphere of the city. Nevertheless, when a rich lawyer who is on a hunting trip offers to take little Harry to New York and send him to school, both Jim Fenton and Harry's father agree that the opportunity for an education cannot be turned down.

The result of all this education is that the rescued children develop into worthwhile and productive people. The qualities that make them worthwhile and productive come from their own efforts. The rescues give the children a chance to develop; the actual development is up to the child. The fact that the children do so well is a clear reflection of the democratic ideal of the self-made man. The respect for what a man can do is far greater than an appreciation of his blood lines. However, the democratic ideal becomes less strong when a potential marriage is involved. Several of the rescued children find their true birth revealed as upper class at the end of the novels. These revelations are all connected to potential marriages. The convention of the rescue of a child, however, reflects clear support for the belief that, given a fair chance, anyone can rise from obscurity on the strength of personal merit.

The rescue of a child contributed to the readers' image of an ideal world in two ways. First, it represented the idea of a positive good in action. In the ideal world all people possess and exercise a sense of right, a sense of human obligation, and a sense of moral values. They do good because they are good. The rescue of a child shows this kind of person in action. No one rescues in expectation of reward. The bond of common humanity is in operation.

The second ideal state reflected by the convention is in the fact that good action is repaid or rewarded in the present. Writers (and obviously the readers) rejected the idea of a good act going unappreciated or unrewarded. The rescuers never regret their actions, and all are pleased with the results.

How clearly the rescue of a child reflected these two ideal states is easily seen in Louisa May Alcott's *Rose in Bloom* (1876). Alcott did not use the rescue convention to structure her novel, and, in fact, its function in the novel is very slight—it is there only to show the factors of goodness and reward.

One day Rose meets her cousin Mac holding "a child of three—so pale, so thin and tiny, that looked like a small scared bird just fallen from the nest."[17] The child's mother has died in a hospital (Mac is studying medicine), and Mac has promised that he will look after the baby. But the job is rather difficult for a single young man. Rose is instantly enthralled with the idea of rescuing the child. "I'm going to take this child home; and, if Uncle is willing, I'll adopt her, and she shall be happy!" (p. 245). Alcott's two good people now have a special tie, and it is not long before they get their reward in love and marriage. Alcott certainly did not need the rescue to get two young people together, but the rescue is a nice way to again emphasize that ideal state—goodness exists and it is always rewarded.

These two ideals seem so important that popular novelists often used a situation in which the child is the one doing the rescuing, a variation of the convention. This variation did not have the developed structure of the full pattern for the rescue of a child, and worked to reflect only that goodness exists naturally in man (who is more naturally good than a child?) and that goodness will be rewarded. The rewards are usually tangible and often immediate.

One of the most popular domestic novels, *Ishmael* (E.D.E.N. Southworth, 1864), used a child as a rescuer. Ishmael Worth may be the most noble character in popular fiction. Southworth tells the reader over and over how good Ishmael is. "Reader! I am not fooling you with a fictitious character here. Do you not love this boy?"[18] When he is about twelve, a fire breaks out at Brudenell Hall. The two Middleton sons are trapped. Ishmael "dashed into the front hall and up the main staircase through volumes of smoke that rolled down and nearly suffocated him" (p. 222). He rescues the boys, and his reward comes at once. He is given an education and a chance to make something of himself. Demonstrating how closely education was believed to be linked with one's future, the old black schoolmaster, who has been tutoring Ishmael, exclaims, "Your everlastin' fortin's made, young Ishmael!" (p. 237). Eventually, Ishmael becomes a lawyer.

A rescue from drowning is used in Thomas Nelson Page's *Gordon Keith* (1903). Twelve-year-old Gordon is dragged from a lake by young Norman Wentworth. The two become lifelong friends, and years later Gordon effects a reconciliation between Norman and his estranged wife. Perhaps even more crucial, Gordon slows a run on Norman's bank by delaying the line and making a deposit, thus impressing the lower class depositors who are trying to take their money out. "I have confidence enough in this bank to put my money here."[19] Norman's rescue of Gordon so many years before brings its reward when he least expects it.

Caleb Wright in 1845 (*Wyoming, a Tale*) also used the situation of a child doing the rescuing. The book opens with eleven-year-old Walter Henderson coming upon an Indian boy caught between some poles and apparently strangled. "Walter seized a rail, and placing one end of it between the poles, exerted a sufficient lever power to break away one of them" (p. 6). The Indian boy survives to become a great chief, and years later he saves Walter from torture and death during the battle of Oriskany. The Indian chief also gives Walter a packet at that time. "Keep it safely; its value some time hereafter may remind you of a friend" (p. 54). Walter's reward is complete when the packet reveals his sweetheart's respectable parentage and facilitates their marriage. The Indian here repays his own rescue quite handsomely and rewards Walter for his actions.

The ideal of what constituted a reward for the child who rescued someone was so well known that Mark Twain could make fun of it. In *The Adventures of Tom Sawyer* (1876), Huck Finn rescues the Widow Douglas who is about to become the victim of a robbery. Just as the pattern dictates, Huck gets an immediate reward. But Mark Twain does not present it quite as the domestic novelists would have:

> His sufferings were almost more than he could bear. The widow's servants kept him clean and neat, combed and brushed.... He had to eat with knife and fork; he had to use napkin, cup, and plate; he had to learn his book; he had to go to church; he had to talk so properly that speech became insipid.[20]

Huck endures his reward but three weeks and then runs away.

Mark Twain's cynical view notwithstanding, the American readers who bought the popular novels did believe that such a life was a reward. A supportive environment and a solid education were the foundation for a happy, useful—and successful—life. Further, by connecting the romantic plot to the rescue of a child, writers could show that everyone who developed a useful, successful life would also develop a satisfying romantic relationship. The pattern for the rescue of a child implied that every child in America could succeed in all things. The reading public wanted to believe it.

Chapter III

The Rescue from Physical Danger

When the heroine of a popular nineteenth century novel found herself in a runaway carriage, she usually had little cause for despair. It was fairly certain that, in a matter of seconds, a handsome young man would rush forward and rescue her. The convention in which a female is rescued from physical danger by a male (both parties were invariably young and attractive) was almost a staple of the popular novel which contained any romantic story at all. Certainly the situation of the pretty young girl in danger and the strong, handsome young fellow rescuing her provided in itself a vicarious thrill for readers. But the rescue from physical danger was also a good way for writers to illustrate the idea of natural sexual roles and the concept that a man's worth was not based on his social level or inheritance alone, but also on his actions.

Although the pattern of the rescue from physical danger is not as clearcut as the pattern for the rescue of a child, the convention, with whatever twist the individual writer chose to give it, had as its basis the solid belief that woman is made to be rescued and man is made to rescue her. In Emerson Bennett's novel *The Forest Rose; A Tale of the Frontier* (1850), this belief is illustrated quite clearly when Bennett introduces the young lovers. Bennett explains that Albert loves Rose because "the object of his affections was physically weak and needed a strong arm."[1] Rose loves Albert because "she could look up to the being of her choice and feel in him a protector" (p. 11). Just to make sure that the reader doesn't miss the point, Bennett comments, "By a righteous law of nature, man loves what he can foster and protect; woman, what can cherish and protect her" (p. 11).

Popular writers were obviously using this idea of the man as natural protector when they included the rescue from physical danger in their romantic plots. The rescue provided an easy way for the writers to establish that this particular man was capable of protecting this particular woman. In a

35

very early American novel, *Monima or The Begger Girl* (Martha Read, 1802), Monima is rescued several times—from the workhouse, from a mugger, and from kidnappers—by an older man who always happens to be walking down the street at precisely the time Monima needs to be rescued. The novel's episodic plot continues until the man's wife dies, and he is free to marry Monima for no clearer reason than that he has rescued her.[2] The episodic, disjointed structure of most of the early novels rarely involved a more sophisticated use of the rescue from physical danger than as a moment of excitement. As popular writers began to develop more defined themes, the rescue from physical danger began to be useful in demonstrating other social attitudes and in adding significantly to the novels' structures.

If we use the social status of the rescuer as the basis for classification of the several patterns of this rescue convention, we can more easily examine how the rescues worked in the novels and what kinds of attitudes they seem to reflect. In a very popular pattern, the young man is on a social level which is inferior to the young lady's—or at least *appears* to be inferior. Because of this disparity in social class, there is no ordinary way for the hero and heroine to get together. The rescue is crucial in that it makes the heroine instantly aware of this man who has just saved her from a life-threatening danger; it establishes the hero's courage, strength, and disregard for himself, all of which then overshadow his low status; it places him in a position to prove his worth to the heroine's protective family; and it seems to indicate that this couple fits what Bennett described as the natural female and male roles of frailty and strength. The rescue from physical danger when the man is socially or financially inferior to the heroine tends to come early in the novel, and, therefore, it opens the way to a development of romance.

James Kirke Paulding's *The Dutchman's Fireside* (1831) illustrates this pattern of the rescue from physical danger. Sybrandt Westbrook is the son of a distant cousin of Catalina Vancour, daughter of a wealthy farmer. Sybrandt is not only very poor, he is so inept and awkward that his manhood is open to question. Here, the hero's heritage is no problem, but his economic status and social problems place him considerably below Catalina.

Catalina is somewhat amused by his awkwardness, and, in a gesture of charity, invites him on an island picnic with some friends. Fortunately for the future of Sybrandt's romance but, unfortunately for the picnickers, a violent storm comes up.

> This storm was for a long time traditionary for its terrible violence; and for more than half a century people talked of the incessant flashes of the lightning, the stunning and harsh violence of the thunder, the deluge of rain, the hurricane which accompanied it, the lofty trees... torn up by the roots....[3]

Sybrandt heroically guides their skiff through the waves when, suddenly, the boat capsizes. Catalina "became insensible the moment the accident occurred and would have quickly perished, had not Sybrandt swum into the edge of the turbulent whirlpool where she was floating, and brought her safely to the land" (p. 66). Sybrandt, battling violent waves to save Catalina from certain death, provides a rather spectacular rescue. In a moment, the rescue has scuttled any lingering questions about Sybrandt's manliness. Although Catalina's interest in Sybrandt has been kindled, her mother still wishes for a better match. Since Catalina is susceptible to her mother's pressures, she does continue to entertain other suitors. This rescue early in the novel has opened the door to romance, but it certainly does not settle all the issues or resolve all parental opposition. Sybrandt's jealousy and Catalina's uncertainty result in a misunderstanding, and Sybrandt goes off to trade on the Indian frontier for a year.

Most popular writers did not allow their lower status heroes to win their ladies after only one rescue. The first rescue early in the novel established the hero's real worth as greater than his social or financial status, but he needed to do more— often he needed to rescue more—before all obstacles to the match disappeared. In Sybrandt's case, he needed to rescue Catalina again.

When he returns from a year on the frontier (his rugged manliness is now thoroughly established), he finds that a drunken renegade Indian is lurking around the Vancour estate seeking revenge against Catalina's father. Sybrandt keeps watch and sees the Indian follow Catalina to a stream:

> He [Sybrandt] saw him look cautiously round in every direction;

> he saw him lay himself down and crawl on his belly, dragging his
> gun after him towards the edge of the precipice, that he might gain
> a full view of his victim below,—and he followed him noiselessly....
> At length the Indian raised himself on his knee, cocked his
> unerring musket, and carried it to his cheek. In an instant it was
> snatched from his grasp.... Catalina, looking up, saw a sight that
> recalled all her tenderness and all her fears (p. 157).

Sybrandt and the Indian struggle at the brink of the precipice,
and the renegade hurtles over the edge. Catalina faints, of
course, but when she revives, all is settled. "Dearest Sybrandt,
I can now see it all.... You were every night on the watch,
guarding me—me—who was accusing you of spending them in
gaming, riot, and seduction..." (p. 159).

This second rescue has erased all Catalina's doubts about
Sybrandt's devotion and has established that he has the
necessary vigilance and strength to protect her. Catalina's
mother is still not happy over the young man's lack of fortune,
and she sends Catalina off to Albany to visit a cousin. There,
Sybrandt is ridiculed by Catalina's cousin and others as being
too rustic. But Catalina remains faithful. "I'd rather be a
happy wife than a titled lady" (p. 208). Sybrandt has to fight
bravely in the French and Indian War before the two can
finally wed, but at the end of the novel he can say, "You are
mine then, Catalina, at last" (p. 286).

Sybrandt has to rescue twice to overcome thoroughly his
low financial status. Jessee Holman's hero William Evermont
(*The Prisoners of Niagara or Errors of Education*) has to rescue
the girl more than once because of his own moral lapses which
strip him of the status the first rescue gives him. William is the
five-year-old orphan who plunged into the Potomac and
rescued two-year-old Zerelda. Along with repaying his own
rescue as a child, this rescue of Zerelda establishes his innate
worth at an early age. Since he is immediately adopted and
raised as Zerelda's cousin, he is on his way to establishing a
social level that might be sufficient for a match.

But when William reaches his teens, he shows a lack of
moral restraint and gets involved in sexual episodes, becoming
"increasingly bold" with both mature women and young girls.
By age seventeen, William is so dissipated that Holman begins
to sprinkle the novel with miscellaneous rescues of young
women to prove that William, although he does not sexually

protect young women, does physically protect them and so has not lost all sense of male chivalry. It is also made clear that William takes advantage of all the sexual opportunities that come his way, but he does not force helpless women into sexual situations. On a brief visit home, William saves Zerelda from a local Indian attack and partially re-establishes his moral standing in her eyes. Unfortunately, William has not yet truly reformed, and it is not long before he is once more seducing young women. The improved status that he gained from the second rescue is almost immediately lost. Holman continues to have his hero rescue young women from death and other terrible fates—continuing to prove that somewhere under William's sexual immorality is the proper masculine protectiveness.

Finally, Zerelda is once more taken prisoner by the Indians. William, who by this time is trying to straighten out his life by fighting Indians with a local regiment, sees Zerelda in the Indian camp. "I raised my eyes and beheld the female captive... it was Zerelda!" (p. 178). Just as Zerelda is about to be raped by an Indian, William rushes up, tomahawks the Indian, and carries the fainting girl away into the woods. They must travel through the woods for several days before reaching civilization. During that time, William demonstrates masculine strength over and over again. This rescue compensates for all William's sins and re-establishes his worth in Zerelda's eyes.

Although Holman's novel goes on through a seemingly endless maze of coincidence and threatened disaster, William's worth, moral strength and ability to protect Zerelda are no longer questioned by either Zerelda or her family. William's low birth is not forgotten but, rather, it seems to make his rescues even more impressive. Zerelda's comment at the end of the novel assures him of her love:

> "Your birth is an honor to the human name: that such merit, such innate nobility should arise from so low an origin. Oh, Evermont, I love you more dearly on account of your humble parentage; because I love you for yourself" (p. 335).

After this declaration of admiration and love by Zerelda, Holman closes the novel by clearing up his hero's mysterious heritage and revealing that he is really heir to a title. This revelation of birth solves the mystery which began the novel. The novel's romantic plot, however, is built around William's three rescues of Zerelda.

An example of how powerful an obstacle social status can be to a romance occurs in E.D.E.N. Southworth's *Ishmael.* The hero, Ishmael Worth, has been proving his good character since he was a child. When he is about seventeen, he falls desperately in love with the beautiful and proud Claudia Merlin. Because of Ishmael's childhood rescue of the Middleton boys, he has been rewarded with an education. The education has improved his future opportunities but not his social status. He is living with his aunt, who is married to the overseer on Claudia's father's plantation. Ishmael's social level seems an insurmountable barrier. Southworth describes Claudia as "the most ingrained little aristocrat that ever lived.... so perfect an aristocrat that she was quite unconscious of being so" (p. 189). As a young girl, Claudia tells her uncle she will never marry "anybody but a lord!" (p. 195).

It is not, however, a lord who rescues her when she is trapped in a runaway carriage. "On rushed the maddened beasts towards the brink of the precipice!" (p. 338). Ishmael grabs the reins and turns the horses at the last minute, but the horses "threw him down and passed, dragging the carriage with them, over his prostrate body!" (p. 338). Claudia is safe, but Ishmael is half-dead—a condition which requires that he be taken to the Merlin house and nursed for many weeks. Thus, the rescue of Claudia brings Ishmael in close contact with her over a period of time, and she begins to return his love. Ishmael's rescue of Claudia impresses Judge Merlin, who feels the young man has unlimited potential. But Claudia's pride cannot bring her to overlook Ishmael's low birth. In an exchange with her father, Claudia stands firm:

"There is nothing to prevent his becoming a gentlemen." [the judge says]

"Oh yes, there is, papa!"

"To what do you allude, my dear?"

"To his—low birth, papa!"

"His low birth? Claudia! Do we live in a republic or not?"

"Ishmael's parents were not respectable! His mother was never married!" (p. 375)

The judge is disappointed but he does not try to persuade Claudia further. It is noteworthy that the judge expresses the American ideal of social rise through personal merit. Claudia, however, adheres to the idea that birth determines a man's social status.

Now, the reader knows that Ishmael is not illegitimate. Therefore if Claudia's pride would let her overlook his apparent lack of respectable background, all would be right in the end. In several of the novels in this study, the young women do worry about the heroes' low birth. But Claudia is the only heroine who is so adamant about the problem of inequality in social class. Southworth is using Claudia's pride to prove a point. Although Ishmael has proved his worth to the others in the novel, Claudia will not relinquish her pride. In the sequel, *Self-Raised* (1876), Southworth shows Claudia regretting her foolish decision, but it is then too late. So here, Southworth uses the convention of the rescue from physical danger to show what a mistake a young woman can make if she ignores the obvious demonstration of nobility that a young man displays in such a rescue.

The difficulties of proving worth beyond one's social class in the popular novels were nothing to the difficulties of proving worth over one's race. However, James Fenimore Cooper, the first American bestselling novelist,[4] used the rescue from physical danger to demonstrate the nobility of a young red man as well as a young white man. Cooper's *The Last of the Mohicans* (1826) probably sold over 2 million copies in the United States alone.[5] The plot structure, as has often been noted, is based on capture/pursuit/rescue, capture/pursuit/-rescue. The sisters Cora and Alice Munro are the young ladies who are rescued, and the men engaged through most of the novel in rescuing them are led by Cooper's famous hero Natty Bumppo. The sisters are traveling to join their father, commander of Fort William Henry, when Cora catches the eye of the Huron Magua, and the continuing chase begins. In spite of the fact that several men are involved, and although the sisters are usually rescued at the same time, the reader knows that Major Duncan Heyward is rescuing Alice, and the Mohican Uncas is rescuing Cora. In one instance, a Huron seizes Cora by her hair:

> He tore her from her frantic hold and bowed her down with brutal
> violence to her knees.... It was just then the sight caught the eye of
> Uncas. Bounding from his footsteps he appeared for an instant
> darting through the air, and descending in a ball he fell on the
> chest of his enemy.... They rose together, fought, and bled... the
> knife of Uncas reached his heart.[6]

Uncas is an Indian, so he does not really have any social status
in the white civilization. But his daring feats of rescue bring
him immediately to almost god-like stature:

> At a little distance in advance stood Uncas, his whole person
> thrown powerfully into view. The travelers anxiously regarded
> the upright, flexible figure of the young Mohican... there was no
> concealment to his dark, glancing, fearless eye, alike terrible and
> calm; the bold outline of his high, haughty features, pure in their
> native red; or to the dignified elevation of his receding forehead,
> together with all the finest proportions of a noble head.... such an
> umblemished specimen of the noblest proportions of man (p. 61).

Cora exclaims, "Who that looks at this creature of nature,
remembers the shade of his skin!" (p. 62). The fact that "an
embarrassed silence" follows this remark indicates that Cora
may forget the shade of Uncas' skin but the others will not. It is
revealed later in the novel that Cora has some black ancestry.
Although Cora and Uncas never learn of her heritage, Cooper
may be implying that Uncas feels an attraction to Cora and
she feels an affinity for him precisely because of her racial
make-up.

The pursuit and rescue pattern goes on, but in the last
desperate rescue of Cora, Uncas becomes reckless. He and Cora
are both killed before Natty can dispose of the villain Magua.
Cooper used the convention of the physical rescue here very
successfully. He presented a male of unquestionably lower
social status who, through daring rescues of the female,
reached an almost super-human level. That Uncas is also
recognized as a leader of his tribe adds to his glamor but does
little for his status in a white society. There is no doubt about
the respect that all the white characters have for Uncas. He is
described at various times as "fearless and generous looking"
(p. 61); as having "eyes that had already lost their fierceness,
and were beaming with a sympathy that elevated him far
above the intelligence, and advanced him probably centuries
before the practices of his nation" (p. 135); and as "the rising

sun" (p. 367). Cooper ended the novel with the tragic deaths of Uncas and Cora because he could not bring himself to use the rest of the rescue pattern and allow Cora and Uncas to marry. Thus, Cooper found himself in the position of having elevated Uncas somewhat through daring exploits but not enough to cross racial lines in marriage. Since Cora is racially mixed, a marriage would mingle three races, a prospect Cooper did not wish to present. The importance of a pure race is emphasized by Natty who lives with the Indians but often says that he is glad he has no Indian blood.

Cooper's contemporary, William Gilmore Simms, also wrote about brave and noble Indians, but he did not use them in his romantic situations. In Simms' novel *The Yemassee* (1835), the romantic plot involves Bess Matthews, daughter of a colonial minister, and her admirer Captain Gabriel Harrison. The problem here is that Harrison does not appear to do anything very substantial for a living, and Bess's father objects to him as a suitor. The reader, however, knows that Harrison is really the governor of Carolina, Lord Craven, and so there is no problem on either a social or financial level. Knowing that the reader will not worry about the appropriateness of the match, Simms builds his plot with adventure upon adventure all leading to Harrison's climactic rescue of Bess.

Bess is the ideal heroine for the rescue from physical danger. She is sweet, lovely, helpless and her sole function in the novel seems to be to provide an object for all the men in the book to rescue. She literally faints at every crisis. She is saved by the Indian Occonestoga when she comes upon a rattlesnake in the woods. "Insensibility came to her aid, and she lay almost lifeless under the very folds of the monster."[7] She is saved by her father when Indians attack their home. " 'God be merciful—oh! my father—oh! Gabriel, save me—Gabriel—Ah! God, God—he cannot—' her eye closed, and she lay supine under the knife of the savage" (p. 286). She is also saved from Indians by the villain Chorley, a pirate. "The terror was too great; for as she beheld the whirling arm and the wave of glittering steel, she closed her eyes, and insensibility came to her relief, while she sank down under the feet of the savage" (p. 291). Since Chorley has an immoral reason for rescuing her, she then needs to be saved from Chorley by her lover Harrison.

" 'Come to me, Gabriel—save me, save me, or I perish. It is I—thy own Bess—ever thine—save me, save me.' She fell back fainting with exhaustion and excitement" (p. 344). As Harrison shoots Chorley and then sweeps Bess out of the bay where she is in danger of drowning, we are told, "She was a child in his grasp, for the strength of his fearless and passionate spirit, not less than that of his native vigour, was active to save her" (p. 346). After such a rescue, it is no wonder that Bess' parents immediately abandon their opposition to Harrison. "It was not long ere she lay in the arms of her parents, whose mutual tears and congratulations came sweetly, along with their free consent, to make her preserver happy with the hand hitherto denied him" (p. 346). The discovery of Harrison's real identity smooths over any parental reservations about the marriage, but the rescue itself earns him Bess' hand in marriage. Certainly, Bess has proved that she needs someone like Harrison to protect her.

Since the readers knew that Harrison did not actually lack social status, Simms could build to the rescue at the end of the novel and resolve all parental objections at once. Most historical romance writers, however, continued to use the rescue as an early event in the romance. The authors at the end of the nineteenth century who wrote historical romances found the rescue pattern very helpful.

Charles Major's *When Knighthood Was in Flower* (1898) was an extremely popular historical romance. The *National Union Catalog* lists a seventeenth edition in 1899, and Hart says the novel sold over 200,000 copies before dropping off the bestseller lists in 1901.[8] The novel, based on the real romance of Henry VIII's sister Mary and Charles Brandon, has the two necessary characters for a good rescue from physical danger. The Princess Mary is of a very high status, and Charles Brandon, a captain in the guard, is definitely beneath her.

Mary teases and flirts with Brandon, but she is very much aware of the gap between them; and "the possibility of such a thing as a union with Brandon had never entered her head."[9] However, one night Mary is out alone with one of her maids visiting a soothsayer when she is attacked by political enemies from the court. Brandon, who has been following her out of concern for her safety, comes to the rescue:

It was but a moment till Brandon came up with the pursuers, who, all unconscious that they in turn were pursued, did not expect an attack from the rear. The men remaining on horseback shouted an alarm to their comrades, but so intent were the latter in their pursuit that they did not hear. One of the men on foot fell dead, pierced through the neck by Brandon's sword, before either was aware of his presence. The other turned but was a corpse before he could cry out (pp. 141-42).

After she is safe again, Mary thinks about the situation:

She still saw the great distance between them as before, but with this difference, she was looking up now. Before that event he had been plain Charles Brandon, and she the Princess Mary. She was the princess still, but he was a demi-god. No mere mortal, thought she, could be so brave and strong and generous and wise; and above all no mere mortal could vanquish odds of four to one (p. 167).

In thinking about their possible future, Mary actually puts it in marketing terms. Surely, he would "win glory and fortune, and then return to buy her from her brother Henry with millions of pounds of yellow gold" (p. 168). Mary obviously feels that Henry will not give up his sister for a mere rescue although the rescue is enough to make Brandon worthy in her eyes. Mary is right about her brother. There are many plot complications before Henry VIII agrees to the marriage. But the rescue settled the question in Mary's eyes, and at the end of the novel she weds her love.

Undoubtedly, the commoner proving that he could take care of the woman who is a member of royalty appealed to Americans proud of their democratic institutions during the century after the Revolutionary War. In Mary Johnston's historical romance *To Have and to Hold* (1900), the heroine is the English king's ward and is being pursued by the lecherous Lord Carnal. She flees to Jamestown, Virginia in 1621, on a shipload of brides for the settlers. The beautiful Jocelyn Leigh is almost immediately in need of rescue as a local ruffian attempts unwelcome liberties. Fortunately, Captain Ralph Percy, a Jamestown settler and therefore representative of the first pioneer stock in America, sees her struggling. "She struggled fiercely, bending her head this way and that, but his hot lips had touched her face before I could come between."[10] Ralph knocks the thug down and sends him off.

Jocelyn is a lady in difficulty. Ralph is attracted to her, so she agrees to marry him because she needs protection from Lord Carnal. But she insists that it be a marriage in name only. "I appeal to your generosity, to your honor" (p. 36). Ralph assures her he is a gentleman—as heroes have to be. So the marriage here is actually part of the rescue. It is Ralph's role now to continue to protect her—and he has to fight off Lord Carnal on several occasions. He must also defy the direct orders of his king. At the end of the novel, Lord Carnal is horribly maimed by a panther and commits suicide. Ralph's continuing rescues of Jocelyn have moved her through the stages of gratitude and respect to love. She becomes Ralph's loving wife at the end of the novel. "With all my heart I love thee, my knight, my lover, my lord and husband" (p. 398). There is no doubt that Ralph is worthy of her and capable of protecting her. This novel had record sales for five months and sold nearly 250,000 copies.[11] The entire plot was based on the convention of the rescue from physical danger. The first rescue introduced the couple. The larger rescue—marrying to discourage Lord Carnal—required constant reinforcement throughout the plot until the danger was over. At the end, Jocelyn knows that Ralph's merits override his commoner status.

Another historical romance was the turn-of-the-century hit *Beverly of Graustark* (George McCutcheon, 1904). Beverly, a dynamic, fearless, and independent American girl, is on her way to visit her friend Princess Yetive of Graustark. Her coach drivers desert her, and she is stranded in the mountains with only a servant. They are picked up by mountain bandits who promise to guide them to Graustark. The leader of the band is Baldos the goat herder, who seems to be a cut above the others. That night, a mountain lion enters their cave and attacks Beverly. Baldos intercepts the beast. "The lion's gaunt body shot through the air. In two bounds he was upon the goat-hunter."[12] Baldos fights the animal off with a dagger and saves Beverly. She is impressed. "He's a man, if there ever was one. Don't let me hear you call him a goat puncher again," she tells her servant (p. 67). Again, the rescue proves the man's ability to protect the woman, and his status rises immediately because of his courage. Other adventures follow, and Baldos continues to prove courage, daring and resourcefulness. When at the end of the novel, he tells Beverly, "You will not give yourself to the lowly, humble hunter," she answers "I will marry you, Paul. I love you" (p. 314). The fact that Baldos turns out to be Prince Dantan of Dawsbergen makes everything better at the end, but it was the rescue that won Beverly's admiration and then her love.

Although the writers of historical romances continued to have their heroines rescued from certain death—or worse—a trend seems to have developed around the turn of the century in which the convention continues to use a man of low social status and a woman of high status, but the rescue in the novel is from a physical danger of a more minor nature than earlier in the century.

In Owen Wister's novel *The Virginian* (1902), Molly Stark Wood, a teacher from an old Vermont family, is on a stage going to Medicine Bow, Wyoming when "two wheels sank down over an edge, [of the river bank] and the canvas toppled like a descending kite. The ripple came sucking through the upper spokes and... she felt the seat careen...."[13] Molly's predicament is eased when "a tall rider appeared close against the buried axles, and took her out of the stage on his horse so suddenly that she screamed... and found herself lifted down upon the shore" (p. 101).

This rescue is hardly life saving, but it fits the pattern by introducing the hero and heroine and sparking her interest and appreciation at once. "Miss Wood entertained... maidenly hope to see him again" (p. 103). Molly is very conscious of their differences in education and social status. She starts to improve the Virginian's education, giving him books to read while telling him that she could not love him because of social differences. But as "the slow cowpuncher unfolded his notions of masculine courage and modesty," Molly lets her class consciousness slip away (p. 348). Although she objects to the brutal frontier code of justice, she accepts his participation in it:

> By love and her surrender to him their positions had been exchanged. He was not now... her half-obeying, half-refractory worshipper. She was no longer his half-indulgent, half-scornful superior. Her better birth and schooling...had given way before the onset of the natural man himself. (p. 447-9)

The rescue here does not dispel any of the disparity in social level, but it provides the opportunity for the Virginian to show his worth and earn Molly's respect.

Another novel of frontier justice was *The Lone Star Ranger* (1914) by Zane Grey, called one of America's five most popular writers in the first quarter of the twentieth century.[14] Grey used the rescue pattern to bring romance to his hero Buck Duane, a fugitive from a murder charge. Offered a pardon if he works under cover for the Texas Rangers, Buck is to investigate the dangerous town of Fairdale and its mayor Colonel Longstreth. Buck meets Longstreth's daughter Ray when he and the Colonel intercept a robber who is ripping Ray's dress off. Buck shoots the robber. "You saved my life," cries Ray, and the rescue pattern is underway.[15] Actually, Buck realizes that the Colonel's arrival probably saved Ray, but the rescue not only introduces him to a pretty girl, but puts him in a position to carry out his investigation. At the end of this novel, Buck's status is elevated because he has earned his pardon while Ray's status actually falls when her father is exposed as a crook.

In Thomas Nelson Page's *Gordon Keith* the hero rescues Alice Yorke when he finds her thrown from her horse and unconscious. Gordon carries her down the hill and revives her. Again, this physical rescue is not as dramatic as the rescues in the earlier novels or the historical romances, but it serves to demonstrate Gordon's inner worth. Gordon is from an old Southern family, but the Civil War ruined the family's fortunes. When he meets Alice, he is a poor and shabby schoolmaster; but Alice tells her mother firmly, "He is a gentleman" (p. 88). However, mother prevails and whisks Alice off to New York and a wealthy marriage. The rescue convinces Alice of Gordon's merit, but it does not impress Mrs. Yorke. By the time Gordon can improve his financial situation and prove himself in the business world, it is too late. Page's use of the first part of the rescue convention illustrates just how wrong Mrs. Yorke is in her opposition to Gordon only on financial grounds. Page does not emphasize the folly of opposition of grounds of finance as much as Southworth does the folly of opposition on grounds of birth, but he makes his point nevertheless.

In all these books, a young man of apparently inferior social status is given a chance to rescue a young lady and thereby demonstrate his inherent nobility and courage. In a few novels, the writer uses the rescue from physical danger to break down an ideological difference between the young man and the girl's family. In those cases, it is not the social status but the political beliefs that separate the couple. Since the girl already loves the young man and since the social status is not a problem, the rescue does not act as introduction or an impetus toward upward social movement. In this situation, the hero rescues a relative of the heroine, someone who is opposing the match. The rescue is at the end of the novel and works as the only thing that can overcome the obstacle to the romance.

Clear examples of this use of the rescue pattern occur in Albion W. Tourgée's *A Fool's Errand* (1879) and John Fox Jr.'s *The Little Shepherd of Kingdom Come*. Tourgée's novel is concerned with Reconstruction in North Carolina. Yankee Republican Colonel Comfort Servosse buys a plantation, brings his family south, and becomes politically active. The focus of the novel is on Servosse and his political activities, including his anti-Klan and pro-black positions. However, Servosse does have a lovely daughter, Lily, who falls in love with Melville Gurney, the son of General Gurney, ex-Confederate officer. Both families oppose any thought of a match. Political strife continues, and an anonymous warning arrives, saying that the Klan intends to ambush Servosse on his way home from the railroad station. Lily is alone when the warning comes, but she knows that she must do something to save her father:

> Before the horse was saddled, Lily had donned her riding-habit, put a revolver in her belt... swallowed a hasty supper, scrawled a short note to her mother... and was ready to start on a night-ride to Glenville.[16]

Glenville is sixteen miles away, and Lily rides frantically. "I will save him. O God, help me! I am but a weak girl" (p. 277). Around a turn she rides right into a meeting of the Klan. Hiding, she eases away to a bend in the road where she sees "sitting before her in the moonlight, one of the disguised horsemen, evidently a sentry" (p. 282). Moving quickly, Lily

> shot like an arrow into the bright moonlight, straight toward the black muffled horseman. "My God!" he cried, amazed at the

> sudden apparition. She was close upon him in an instant. There
> was a shot; his startled horse sprang aside and Lily... was flying
> down the road toward Glenville (p. 282).

Lily reaches the train station and warns her father, saving him from ambush.

It would appear from this description that the rescue certainly must be credited to Lily, and she becomes a local heroine after the event. But we find that the sentry she shot was Melville Gurney, who recognized her as she rode past him. When the other Klan members reach him, he tells them that a rabbit startled him and he shot himself. So Melville supports Lily's ride and, in fact, prevents her from getting caught as she surely would have been without his help. Melville, of course, as a gentleman, cannot claim credit for himself, so a friend makes sure Servosse hears the whole story:

> "Melville Gurney's chivalry and presence of mind is what saved
> you—next, of course, to Miss Lily's heroism.... But if Melville
> Gurney had not put him off the scene... you would have had Jake
> Carver and the rest on you" (pp. 349-50).

Servosse responds, "My God! You are right! I had never thought of it in that way" (p. 350). Servosse immediately writes to Melville and thanks him. When Melville responds by asking if he may court Lily, Servosse answers, "You are entirely unobjectionable to me" (p. 355). Melville's participation in the rescue inspires not only a feeling of personal gratitude in Servosse, but also a realization that the young man is honorable and possesses a sense of justice. Since the Klan has now broken up and since Melville had not been deeply involved in its activities, the rescue erases all Servosse's objections. Lily still insists on waiting for General Gurney's approval—an approval which takes somewhat longer—before she and Melville can wed.

The rescue in this case has to surmount objections to the young man's fundamental beliefs, a far more difficult task than just giving him an opportunity to prove his good personal qualities. Fox's novel, set in Kentucky, contains much the same problem in that Chad, after being taken in as an orphan by Major Buford, has stunned all those close to him by joining the Union army. Chad loves Margaret Dean, and he no sooner finds out that she loves him in return than the war breaks out, and his conscience directs him to join the Yankees. He leaves, having alienated Margaret's family. But later when Chad learns that Margaret's brother Dan is going to be shot as a guerilla, he rides a desperate sixty miles to try to reach the commandant and get a stay of execution. "Twenty-seven miles to go and less than three hours before sunrise..." (p. 272). As dawn comes, Chad arrives with the stay of execution at the same time the rebels are defeating the Union forces and freeing the prisoners. Chad's rescue was needed only if the rebels had not won the battle, but he got the stay of execution and completed his ride, thus symbolically rescuing Dan. When Dan is a prisoner at the end of the war, Chad nurses him back to health and brings him home. Because of these rescues, at the war's end Mrs. Dean greets Chad with warmth:

> "I owe my son's life to you, Captain Buford," said Mrs. Dean with trembling lip, "and you must make our house your home while you are here. I bring that message to you from Harry and Margaret. I know and they know now all that you have done for us and all you have tried to do" (p. 320).

All opposition is over, and Margaret is Chad's. He cannot take the offered happiness because of another rescue convention—the female rescuing the male. The point in both Fox's and Tourgée's novels is that a heroic rescue of a male relative of the young lady can crumble family opposition which is based on political differences. The young man has shown that he can overlook political considerations when the humanitarian need arises, and the family must do likewise.

In considering how this convention of the rescue from physical danger generally works in the novels, we should keep in mind that we are dealing with what were regarded as the natural female and male roles. Although some of the young women may have a bit too much pride, all of them are perfect examples of women who deserve to be rescued. However, when a writer uses a hero who is morally superior to the young lady, he seems to have difficulty in deciding where to place the rescue. One writer who specialized in strict moral issues was E. P. Roe, a Presbyterian minister. Roe's books were fantastically successful. Ten years after the first printing of *Barriers Burned Away* (1872), a "limited" edition of 100,000 copies sold out immediately.[17]

Roe's novel starts out by introducing Dennis Fleet, a poor young man trying to support a mother and two sisters by working as a porter in an art gallery. He falls in love with Christine Ludolph, the daughter of the gallery owner. "It should seem that circumstances brought the threads of these two lives near each other... the most impassable barriers rose between them.... She was the daughter of the wealthy aristocratic Mr. Ludolph; he was her father's porter."[18] Dennis does have an education but no wealth. He tells Christine, "I am sufficiently a democrat, Miss Ludolph, to believe that a man can be a man in any honest work." "And I, Mr. Fleet," she replies, "am not in the least degree a democrat" (p. 123).

Here is an obvious situation where we need a physical rescue to break down Christine's pride. But Roe's novel includes the fact that Dennis is a devout Christian, and Christine is an "unbeliever in God and religion" (p. 83). Dennis then is morally superior to Christine, and her conversion must take place before she is worthy of being rescued. In the novel, Dennis becomes a successful artist, so there is no financial barrier to the match. The barrier is Christine's lack of faith in God. Roe uses the rescue from physical danger at the end of the novel to push Christine into accepting the Christian faith.

When the Chicago fire breaks out, Dennis (while saving other people along the way) rushes to rescue Christine. "Can you save me? Oh, do you think you can save me?" "Yes, I feel sure I can," Dennis answers calmly (p. 368). While they desperately struggle to reach Lake Michigan ahead of the fire, Dennis performs one heroic feat after another, and Christine begins to think that "he was right and she was wrong" (p. 376). While the fire rages, the two huddle in Lake Michigan. By the time the fire subsides, Christine has been converted. She asks, "And can you still truly love me after all the shameful past?" "When have I ceased to love you?" Dennis replies, and all ends well (p. 433).

This rescue ends the novel. Dennis has already improved his financial status. The rescue proves that he is physically capable of caring for Christine. More important for Roe's theme, however, the rescue demonstrates the strength of Christian action and results in Christine's conversion, thus making her worthy of being rescued—and worthy of marrying an honest Christian man.

It would seem that this question of whether the young lady was worthy of being rescued also bothered John Esten Cooke when he wrote *The Virginia Comedians or Old Days in the Old Dominion* (1854). Early in the novel, Beatrice Hallam is out sailing when she falls overboard:

> The young man in the skiff... seemed to have recognized the young woman—and uttering an exclamation which was drowned in the shrill blast, threw himself into the waves, and catching her half-submerged form as she rose, struck out with the ease of a practiced swimmer.[19]

The immediate result of this rescue is love. "Beatrice Hallam felt her face fill with blood, her heart throb: for the first time she had found the nature which heaven had moulded in the form of her own" (p. 91). The difficulty Cooke faced at this point was that, although Charles Waters is a poor farmer of "humbler class" (p. 90), Beatrice is an actress, placing her even lower on the social ladder. Cooke has used the rescue for introduction and to stimulate love, but there is a disturbing possibility that Beatrice may not be worthy of rescue—although we do know that she has been fighting off the immoral advances of Champ Effingham. This problem of the woman's worth may be one of the reasons Cooke soon reveals that Beatrice is really Charles' cousin. The revelation of birth allows Beatrice to give up the stage and makes the two young people of equal social status. To clearly emphasize the natural roles, now perfectly suitable, Cooke shows Beatrice being kidnapped by the lustful Champ. As they speed off in a coach, Charles follows. "He now felt the advantages of his country training—days and nights spent in hunting; his speed was scarcely less than that of the flying horse" (p. 310). Although wounded, this amazingly fast young man foils the abduction and rescues Beatrice. This second rescue serves to demonstrate that it is Charles who has the right to rescue Beatrice and that Beatrice is worthy of rescue. They are filling natural male and female roles.

By mid-century, most of the popular writers apparently used the convention of the rescue from physical danger as a quick way to demonstrate the inherent worth of the lower class hero so that he could begin to prove his abilities in other areas. Before that time, however, writers frequently had men rescue women of their own class. The convention, then in its early stages, was used as a symbol of the divine correctness of these two people marrying. The young woman is being rescued by the man most suited to care for her. The fact that he is the one to perform the rescue seems to prove that he is the one fated to protect her for the rest of their lives.

Cooper uses this approach with the second couple in *The Last of the Mohicans*. Socially Major Duncan Heyward is a perfect match for Alice Munro. What Duncan must prove with his rescues of Alice is that he is capable of caring for her in the wilderness, the new American civilization. Since Alice trembles and faints at every crisis, there is no doubt that she needs someone to look out for her. Duncan learns from Natty how to survive in the wilderness and proves he can indeed protect Alice who is frequently referred to in the novel as a "child."

Alice may be more childlike than some other heroines, but it is this helpless female frailty which the rescue convention stresses when the writer uses a rescuer of the same social class as the woman. Emerson Bennett carefully explained feminine frailty and masculine strength in *The Forest Rose*. Bennett uses the rescue to illustrate this frailty and strength when Rose is captured by Indians. Albert rescues her and modestly explains, "It was from here I saw you, my own Forest Rose, a helpless prisoner; it was from here I aimed the deadly weapon to set you free; and it was from here I rushed exultingly to clasp you..." (p. 49).

When Rose is captured a second time, Albert vows, "I will either set her free, alone and unaided, or die in the attempt" (p. 63). Albert's role as a lover, then, is to rescue Rose, although it takes him nearly two years to find her before he can rescue her the second time. The plot of this adventure, combined with the opening statements about male and female roles and the two rescues, reinforce the idea that the right man must rescue the right woman.

Two early novels with highly improbable plots based almost entirely on coincidence use the physical rescue in the romantic situations merely to emphasize that these two young people are really right for each other. In Samuel Woodworth's *The Champions of Freedom, or The Mysterious Chief* (1816), George Willoughby rescues his childhood sweetheart

Catherine Fleming from a theater fire. In the confusion, Catherine does not realize George was the one who rescued her, and she allows Thomas Sandford to court her because he claims to be her rescuer. When he makes improper advances, she dismisses him. "The debt was cancelled, and she forbade him her sight."[20] She learns who really rescued her, and everything is straightened out. This mixup is important because it illustrates that, even as early as 1816, the idea had become established that a woman may assume that her rescuer is destined to be her suitor.

The other early novel is James McHenry's *The Betrothed of Wyoming* (1830) in which Henry Austin rescues Agnes Watson from Indians, and it is love at first sight. There are no obstacles to the match, and the pair become engaged. McHenry also has Henry dash to Agnes' aid at the end of the novel when the villain threatens a fate worse than death. This final rescue only affirms what the first rescue began—the right man has found the right woman.

The first dime novel, *Malaeska; the Indian Wife of the White Hunter* (1860) by Ann Sophia Stephens, is concerned primarily with the life of Malaeska. But Stephens uses a rescue from physical danger early in the novel for the purpose of establishing the proper roles of the young lovers Arthur Jones and Martha Fellows. The two have had a lover's quarrel, and Martha is walking alone in the woods when she is seized by Indians. "A dark form rushed from its covert in the brushwood, and rudely seized her, darting back into the wilderness" (p. 47). At once, Arthur rescues her. "That moment a bullet whistled by her cheek. The Indian... staggered back, and fell to the ground..."(p. 47).

Martha realizes instantly that this incident has settled the roles the two are to fill. "Oh, Arthur! dear Arthur, I am glad it was you that saved me," she cries (p. 48). When she apologizes for their earlier quarrel, Arthur forgives her with a "look that humbled her to the heart," and after they are wed, Martha never dares to "brave" that look again (p. 49). The rescue here shows Arthur's superior strength and reaffirms the natural roles, settling the question of who is in charge of the relationship.

One late example of the use of the rescue only to establish traditional roles is in Harold MacGrath's *The Adventures of*

Kathlyn (1914). This novel offers a collection of crises which are stunning in their frequency and intensity. Heroine Kathlyn Hare, an American girl, has a series of adventures in India, putting her almost continually at the point of death or at the mercy of the lustful Umballa. John Bruce, a socially acceptable, immensely capable, and very wealthy white hunter, rescues Kathlyn no less than eight times. Since there is no problem of unequal social levels or parental opposition, MacGrath seems to be using the physical rescue only to stress the inevitable coming together of this extraordinary young man and this extraordinary young woman. MacGrath praises Kathlyn's endurance. "An ordinary woman would have died from mere exhaustion."[21] John's strength impresses Kathlyn. "How strong he was," she sighs (p. 145). By the time John has rescued her eight times (and her father once), there is certainly no doubt that this is a match engineered by fate.

Since the convention of a young man rescuing a young woman from physical danger appears so continuously in popular fiction from the early novels to World War I, it seems obvious that readers enjoyed it. The convention often appears to reflect a definite belief that a young man of low social class may well demonstrate his inherent qualities of chivalry and courage through the rescue. Once the man shows his merit, he may start to rise in the world through his own efforts and finally win the young lady in marriage. Certainly this whole idea shows the American ideal of the self-made man who rises through his own resourcefulness.

In these novels, it is important that the young lady exhibit proper appreciation of all the values that the man has displayed in these rescues. No matter what is finally revealed about the young man's background, the young woman must always agree to marry him before she knows anything more about his ancestry. This acceptance of him proves her own solid moral foundation. Southworth's novel stresses over and over again that Claudia is condemning herself to a loveless life because she will not recognize the virtues displayed in the rescue as more appropriate to happiness than mere money and background.

However, a significant number of novels in this sample also use the plot conventions of the revelation of good birth or of concealed identity in the denouement of the romantic situation. That so many writers felt it safer to equalize the social levels in a traditional way really indicates a doubt about the efficacy of mere deeds to equalize social levels. The revelation of good birth or high status may have created a sigh of relief among readers who felt just a bit uneasy about a nameless nobody marrying the banker's daughter.

Jessee Holman in 1810 clears up the question of William Evermont's birth at the end of *The Prisoners of Niagara or Errors of Education*. William's love, Zerelda, has already vowed that she loves him for himself and says his low birth makes his courage especially impressive. Suddenly William is revealed to be the son of Sir William Valindon. At once, this hero rises to a position in the aristocracy, making him much more suitable for the daughter of a wealthy merchant. The revelation of titled ancestry is particularly interesting in a novel in which the hero joins Washington's army in the Revolutionary War. Holman undercuts his own emphasis on democratic ideals with this story of William's birth.

A birth revelation halfway through the novel occurs in Fox's *The Little Shepherd of Kingdom Come*. As a young boy, Chad has been taken in by Major Buford. The Major suspects very soon that Chad may be the descendant of his grandfather's only brother who had been supposedly killed by Indians in 1778. But there is no proof, and he dismisses the idea. Although the major's friends and neighbors welcome the little boy, Chad reaches an age where his friendship with Margaret Dean causes her parents concern. "It was right that they should be kind to the boy... but they could not have even the pretense of more than a friendly intimacy between the two" (p. 173). Because of Margaret's parents' objections to him, Chad investigates in the mountains and finds that he is indeed related to the major. In spite of all the sterling qualities Chad the orphan had demonstrated up to this time, this revelation of birth puts him in a new and better position:

> It was then that the Major took Chad by the shoulders roughly, and with tears in his eyes, swore he would have no more nonsense from the boy; that Chad was flesh of his flesh and bone of his bone; that he would adopt him..... And it was then that Chad told him how gladly he would come, now that he could bring him an untarnished name (p. 177).

Soon after this incident, Chad is invited to Margaret's home for dinner when, only a few weeks before, her parents had preferred that she stay away from him.

E.D.E.N. Southworth conceals Ishmael's birth from the characters in the novel but not from the readers. Therefore, when Ishmael falls in love with Claudia Merlin, the readers could relax, knowing that the pair's social levels were really equal. Ishmael is the son of Nora Worth, who died after his birth. What the world does not know is that Nora was secretly married to rich Herman Brudenell, whose family owns vast estates in Maryland. Brudenell is wandering through Europe under the impression that he has provided for the boy. Since the characters in Southworth's novel do not find out the truth, however, Claudia's pride stands in the way of romance. Southworth comments that even if Ishmael's parentage were made known and cleared up, "Claudia Merlin, in her present mood of mind, would have died and seen him die, before she would have given her hand to one upon whose birth a single shade of reproach was even suspected to rest" (p. 370). The implications in this novel are complex. Southworth is clearly proving a point with Claudia's obstinacy. Although she admits to loving Ishmael, Claudia marries another solely because of a desire to enter aristocracy. Yet Southworth blunts the issue of love versus ambition because Ishmael is really well born. Perhaps Southworth felt that if Ishmael possessed a good name as well as all his virtues readers would be more upset at the mistake Claudia makes. The fact of Ishmael's birth does work to magnify Claudia's mistake, and in the sequel it makes her disappointment especially bitter. But that fact also reduces the importance of all Ishmael's sterling qualities, which he demonstrates through his actions.

Sometimes a writer uses a concealed identity to cover the fact that the young man's social level is equal to or better than the young lady's. Simms' novel *The Yemassee* has Lord Charles Craven, the governor of Carolina, masquerading as the trader Gabriel Harrison. The reader knows who he is, but Bess' parents do not, and they disapprove of Harrison. Pastor Matthews' attitude toward Harrison has "something of backwardness, a chilly repulsiveness in the manner" (p. 51). When Harrison rescues Bess at the end of the novel, her parents thankfully consent to the match. They are glad to have someone who can protect her. "She is yours, Captain Harrison—she is yours! But for you,.. I dread to think, what would have been her fate" (p. 354). All the same, when Harrison reveals that he is really Governor Craven, there is an extra measure of relief in the pastor's shout of "gratification," and Bess has a "heart full of silent happiness" (p. 357).

In *Beverly of Graustark*, Beverly is very relieved when the goat herder Baldos reveals that he is Prince Dantan. Although she loves him and has agreed to marry him, Beverly has frequently wished Baldos were really a prince. Becoming a princess will be more fun and more respectable than becoming the wife of a goat herder. And, probably, rich American girls should not really marry peasants.

If we consider how many of the novels in this sample used the physical rescue between members of the same class and then how many others used the revelation of birth or identity to equalize the social classes of the lovers, we are left with only a few novels in which the writer depended entirely on the rescue and the future success of the hero to equalize the social levels. The exceptions include Roe, whose theme was the superiority of the Christian life over any social status, and Wister, whose theme was the superiority of Western rugged manliness over Eastern effete culture.

Although the heroines proclaim complete respect for the hero and vow true love, it is impossible to ignore the implications in the endings of these novels. If writers used other kinds of equalizers before the couple could marry, then readers must have felt more comfortable with these traditional signs of worth. This acceptance of the importance of birth reveals a lack of faith in the democratic ideal of a man proving himself through his actions. Since the convention of the child rescue seems to indicate a strong belief in individual development, we must speculate that readers felt less comfortable with this ideal in romantic situations. For marriage, readers seem to have wanted some traditional signs of acceptability and substance. There is no indication in popular novels that it is good birth that makes a character willing to rescue others. Often good Indians rescue white settlers; good people of the lower classes rescue others. It is in the romantic situations, apparently, that writers and presumably the readers felt just a bit uncomfortable when a man's own achievements were the only criteria for marrying into the upper class. Another reason for the reluctance to rely on demonstrated merit may be the tradition that a woman may marry upward, but a man does not unless he is a fortune hunter.

In spite of this seeming preference for traditional proof of respectability, there are some definite social values reflected in the physical rescue situation. The further worthy qualities displayed by the young men after the initial rescue include such things as honesty, courage, fortitude and strength. There are two other specific areas in which the young men usually excel. The first is participation in war or support of country.

One of the ways in which Holman's hero makes up for his sexual immorality is by joining George Washington's army and proving his bravery under fire. McHenry's hero, Henry Austin, also fights in the Revolutionary War. Woodworth's hero George Fleming fights in the War of 1812. Both Cooper and Paulding involve their heroes in the French and Indian War, and, of course, Fox's hero joins the Union army during the Civil War. All these men serve faithfully, valiantly and prove themselves superior to their fellow soldiers. And, of course, the heroes all serve on the "right" side. The villains invariably serve on the opposite side or, worse, become renegades.

If we extend the term war to include any defense of one's country and its values, we can add other heroes to this list of warriors. Both Johnston's and Major's heroes support their kings even though Charles Brandon unadvisedly loves his king's sister and Ralph Percy unadvisedly loves his king's ward. McCutcheon's hero Prince Dantan is engaged throughout the novel in overthrowing evil, repressive Prince Gabriel and recovering his rightful place as ruler of Dawsbergen.

The western novel usually presents patriotism in a somewhat regional context. Both Owen Wister and Zane Grey involve their heroes in the defense of frontier law and order although, in each case, it seems that the hero's defense may jeopardize his romance. This defense of law and order is the precursor of support for the civilized structure of the country and is as important as serving in a war.

Indian fighting was also considered a highly patriotic endeavor. Simms' hero Lord Craven is in disguise because he is investigating and trying to avert Indian uprisings in colonial Carolina. Bennett's hero Albert joins an old Indian fighter while he pursues his sweetheart Rose. It is interesting that Bennett explains that Albert is still "a high-souled, well-born, well-bred young man... who if he were a hunter of men, was rather so from powerful circumstances than from any natural inclination" (p. 69). The point is made that Albert kills Indians but does not scalp them. It is evident from the activities of all these heroes that a worthy young man does serve and support his country—and in an appropriately noble fashion, never sinking to the level of the enemy.

The other major area in which these young men excel is in their work or in earning a living. Heroes in American novels do not lead idle lives. Many are farmers. Cooper's and Major's heroes are in the military, and we also have such exotic occupations as white hunter and prince.

Southworth, Page, Roe and Wister all take their heroes from obscurity and poverty to great financial success. Ishmael becomes a successful lawyer, so honest that he will refuse a case if the client is in the least guilty. Page's Gordon Keith becomes a prominent engineer and then a mine owner. Wister's Virginian has purchased coal land and is planning future success. Roe's Dennis Fleet goes from being a clerk in an art gallery to being a respected artist. The details of these financial rises take up sizeable portions of the novels, showing that such delineation of movements from rags to riches were interesting.

Several of the heroes have yet to reach their full potential wealth at the conclusions of the books, but there is no doubt that such wealth will be realized. Paulding's Sybrandt Westbrook has just returned home from the French and Indian War. But since the uncle who adopted him has died, Sybrandt's inheritance offers possibilities for growth and success. Grey's hero earns a governor's pardon by breaking up the outlaw gang and, at the end of the novel, heads for a new life in Louisiana. Fox's hero heads west with no money but a "strong body and a stout heart" (p. 336). In none of these novels is there any hint that the reader needs to worry about the future. These men are strong and honest and will make their way in the world.

The only novel in which the hard work ethic is not stressed is in Holman's 1810 book. Since William is revealed to be a titled young man, perhaps Holman felt his financial situation was strong enough. Most probably, the importance of titles was still strong enough in the early nineteenth century to ensure success for a young man having one.

The evidence of a strong emphasis on honest work in these novels shows that readers believed not only that the man must earn his own way in the world but also that he must be capable of supporting the woman he has rescued. The man must prove in the rescue that his character is worthy of the woman, and then he must prove himself capable of caring for her both physically and financially.

The female role is clear. She needs the man's protection. She needs to be rescued. Once rescued, she is the reward for the man's bravery, and she has a strong sense of the debt she owes the man. It is another internal contradiction in the rescue convention that while the man proves himself worthy of the woman, she and often her family think of the relationship as a "debt" she owes him. Catalina thinks often of what she owes Sybrandt. She turns down an admirer because of her feeling for Sybrandt. "I have reason to love him; he twice saved my life" (*The Dutchman's Fireside*, p. 217). Princess Mary tells Charles Brandon, "I owe you my life and more—and more a thousand times" (*When Knighthood Was in Flower*, p. 144). Bess' father gives her to Harrison immediately after she is rescued. "It was not long ere she lay in the arms of her parents, whose mutual tears and congratulations came sweetly, along with their free consent, to make her preserver happy with the hand hitherto denied him" (*The Yemassee*, p. 346).

The real attitude being emphasized is that the man has earned a reward, and the woman he rescues is the reward. When a young woman is rescued by a villain, the man usually makes immoral demands. These demands prove he is no gentleman, and there is no reward. But when the hero rescues and makes no demands, then the woman as reward becomes implicit in the situation.

The correctness of male dominance and female submission is given so much emphasis in the novels that the only conclusion we can draw is that readers accepted these roles without reservations. The contrast of feminine weakness and masculine strength leading to masculine dominance appears on all social levels. When the Princess Mary weds Charles

Brandon (now given a title by King Henry), the novel ends:

> ... this fair, sweet, wilful Mary dropped out of history, a sure token
> that her heart was her husband's throne; her soul his empire; her
> every wish his subject, and her will... the meek and lowly servant
> of her strong but gentle lord and master, Charles Brandon, Duke
> of Suffolk (p. 358).

And Jocelyn says at the end of *To Have and To Hold*, "With all
my heart I love thee, my knight, my lover, my lord and
husband" (p. 398). While Dennis is rescuing Christine during
the Chicago fire, a ruffian enters the house. "Trembling and
half fainting... she cried for Dennis and never did knightly
heart respond with more brave and loving throb to the cry of a
helpless woman than his" (*Barriers Burned Away*, p. 367).
When Beatrice Hallam thanks Charles Waters for saving her
life, his father tells her, "Oh, that's his place—you're a weak
little thing, and couldn't be expected to take care of yourself"
(*The Virginia Comedians*, p. 90).

   This weakness, this frailty, this need to be rescued does not
change in popular novels throughout the nineteenth century
although the popular heroine does change. Late nineteenth
century heroines were much more energetic than the earlier
heroines. Bess Matthews does nothing but scream and faint in
The Yemassee in 1835. Kathlyn Hare in *The Adventures of
Kathlyn* in 1914 is a dynamo of activity. Kathlyn has a "gift"
for soothing wild animals. At one point, she faces down a lion.
Threats from tigers do not even worry her. "It seemed to her...
that a film of steel had grown over her nerves" (p. 115). Her
lover, John Bruce, admires her as a woman who "was of the
breed which produces heroes" (p. 155). In spite of her obvious
energy and strength, Kathlyn needs to be rescued eight times
while she sighs over John's superior strength. Heroines may
become fiery, but they still need to be rescued, and they respond
just as the early heroines do, with complete submission to the
man's strength. The woman's positions in relation to the men
they are destined to wed do not change no matter what else
may change in the figure of the young heroine.

   The social attitudes reflected by the rescue from physical
danger of a woman by a man are frustratingly inconsistent. On
the one hand, the young man proves his worth by his daring

rescue. On the other hand, the writers often equalize the social classes through traditional means just in time to prevent the heroines from marrying beneath themselves. Both Page's and Southworth's novels specifically condemn the snobbery about finances or birth that the other writers seem to be bowing to, but Southworth's hero is also revealed as well born. The rescue seems to indicate that the woman is the automatic reward for the man's daring; he dominates through physical strength. Yet it is clear that financial success and the ability to support the woman are really crucial in securing the marriage. The man must prove his ability in these areas.

In spite of these apparent contradictions in the actual social attitudes readers held, the physical rescue does reflect a consistent ideal view of romantic situations. The right man will find the right woman and they will marry. The physical rescue is the test by which we know the ideal couple, the two fated to meet and love. The right man rescues the right woman. The fact that the rescue situation is often the introduction for the couple only intensifies this feeling of destiny in the rescue situation. The rescue in one moment brings together a woman who needs rescuing and a man capable of doing so. The traditional male and female roles are filled immediately, and the rescue seems to show a predestined coming together. In the ideal world, there are no mismatches. The physical rescue is so important in demonstrating which man is suited for which woman that a realist like William Dean Howells uses the convention to avoid a mismatch in his novel *Indian Summer* (1886).

In the novel, Theodore Colville, a forty-one-year-old publisher, is engaged to marry twenty-year-old Imogene Graham. Colville worries somewhat about the age difference, but he decides that it doesn't matter. While Colville, Imogene, Mrs. Bowen, her daughter Effie, and Reverend Morton are all out on a carriage ride, there is trouble with the horses:

> Mrs. Bowen's horses... reared at the sight of the sable crew [a herd of black pigs], and backing violently up-hill, set the carriage across the road, with the hind wheels a few feet from the brink of the wall.[22]

Colville begins to rescue all the women. "Jump, Mrs.

Bowen! jump, Effie! Imogene—" (p. 253). Mrs. Bowen and Effie jump, but Imogene refuses to let Colville rescue her. "The girl sat still, staring at him with reproachful, with disdainful eyes" (p. 253). She lets Reverend Morton pull her out of the carriage. Colville is hurt by the horses. During his subsequent recovery, Imogene tells her mother that she knows now that she likes Colville but does not love him. The engagement ends. The fact that Imogene will not allow Colville to rescue her makes it obvious that he is not the proper man for her. In fact, at the end of the novel, Colville realizes that Mrs. Bowen—who did let him rescue her—is the woman for him. Howells the realist does not go so far as to mate Imogene with Reverend Morton. The fact, however, that Howells uses the convention to reveal that Colville and Imogene are not destined for each other is a significant indication of how important the convention was and how well the readers understood it. In the ideal happy endings of the popular novels, the right man always gets the right woman.

The rescue convention is so clearcut that it can be used as a real life guide. A non-fiction guide for young women aimed at helping them establish romantic relationships with young men includes it. As we would expect, young women are told to be warm, understanding, chaste and adoring. In a chapter designed to give the young woman special advice on how to get the young man to propose marriage, the author recommends "The Rescue Method":

> This is the method used by so many novelists.... In these cases, if the girl will tactfully let the man know of her distress, it is exceedingly hard for him to refrain from comforting her, from trying to make it easy for her, from heroically and chivalrously relieving her of her burdens and taking them upon himself....[23]

This guide for young women was written in 1969 and was in its ninth printing in 1977. Contradictions in its patterns notwithstanding, the rescue convention in the romantic situation is one of our clearest guides to the history of male-female relationships in America.

Chapter IV

The Rescue from a Dilemma

Energetic Kathlyn Hare in Harold MacGrath's 1914 novel, *The Adventures of Kathlyn,* represents a changing emphasis in the American heroine. The change is manifested in an increased physical strength and an increased intellectual development. Early in the novel, Kathlyn singlehandedly captures a runaway lion—demonstrating a remarkable physical presence. She also evaluates John Bruce when she first meets him as a worthwhile man because he caught "her interest in the very fact that he had but little to say and said that crisply and well" (p. 21). That her ability to deal with lions is rare is obvious, but her intellectual appraisal of a man is also a change from early nineteenth century heroines. Early heroines were more apt to sigh over a man's muscles or manners than his intellect. MacGrath does not use these traits in Kathlyn to affect the course of the romantic situation in his novel or to develop a new approach to that situation. In fact, since Kathlyn is rescued from death eight times by Bruce, MacGrath is clearly placing his heroine securely in the traditional female mold. Kathlyn's personal qualities, however, do reflect the change in the popular heroine that began appearing in popular novels in 1875.

All areas of American life were undergoing radical shifts during the last quarter of the nineteenth century. Cities were being swollen by foreign immigrants and migration from the farms. The American frontier closed, and, with the Massacre at Wounded Knee in 1890, the last Indian resistance faded. Labor unions were increasingly violent in their demands. Religious groups, pressured by Darwinism and science, became more liberal and more involved in political and social matters. Politically, Americans were moving from a traditional belief in laissez-faire to a conviction that government should control and regulate. Reform movements developed, and muckrakers called for action to improve social conditions.

The options available to the American woman were also

changing. Several women's colleges opened after the Civil War and, by the end of the century, there were 25,000 students in 128 women's colleges. Work possibilities also expanded because of industrialism. By 1900 some five and a third million women worked outside the home.[1] The percentage of women actually participating in these expanding opportunities was relatively small, and the percentage of women actively in the feminist movement was even smaller; but the ripples of these shifts in attitudes about female roles reached sufficiently deep into the American culture so that at least some popular writers began to reflect the changing concept of the feminine character in their heroines. Cawelti points out that a sympathetic picture of the new woman gradually evolved:

> While the divorcee, the promiscuous, and the prostitute remained beyond the pale and were still usually allocated an unfortunate fate, they were often treated with considerable sympathy and understanding and sometimes were even allowed to take a role as secondary heroines until their tragic fate caught up with them. The official heroine, though still usually characterized by sexual purity, gradually lost much of her submissiveness and was even granted a certain degree of wildness.[2]

The reasons for these changes in the popular heroine stem from the beginnings of the women's movement in America. The Seneca Falls women's rights convention was held in 1848. In 1845, three years earlier, Margaret Fuller, editor of *The Dial*, quarterly magazine of literature, published *Woman in the Nineteenth Century*. In this book, she touched on most of the questions that would be important for feminists later. Central to her ideas is the rejection of the concept that some things are "natural" to women. "I would have Woman lay aside all thought, such as she habitually cherishes, of being taught and led by men. I would have her... dedicate herself to the Sun, the Sun of Truth, and go nowhere if his beams did not make clear the path."[3] Fuller expressed great faith in the ability of women to think for themselves and to handle responsibilities. "Women must leave off asking [men] and being influenced by them, but retire within themselves and explore the ground-work of life till they find their peculiar secret."[4]

Marriage as an institution upset her because, traditionally, the woman was submissive to the man:

> But that is the very fault of marriage, and of the present relation
> between the sexes, that the woman *does* belong to the man,
> instead of forming a whole with him.... Woman, self-centered,
> would never be absorbed by any relation; it would be only an
> experience to her as to man. It is a vulgar error that love, *a* love, to
> Woman is her whole existence; she also is born for Truth and Love
> in their universal energy.[5]

By the last quarter of the nineteenth century, the cumulative effect of the women's movement and the social, economic and religious upheavals in the United States appeared in the characters of heroines in popular novels. Because of these changing concepts of feminine roles and in spite of the unceasing popularity of the rescue from physical danger of the female by the male, another rescue convention appears in the popular novels written after 1875. This convention, tied to the new heroine, is the male's rescue of the female—from a dilemma.

The rescue from a dilemma involves the same components as the physical rescue—a woman in trouble and a man who gets her out of it. The dilemma, however, while it may be serious as a physical danger, requires that the man exhibit not muscles but intellect. The dilemma usually arises less suddenly than the physical danger, and it is more completely part of the entire plot structure. In most cases, the man and woman are on equal social levels, and the rescue occurs at the end of the novel. Since social status is not an issue, the rescue at the end of the novel saves the heroine from her trouble, ends the novel by resolving the problem, and secures the marriage of the couple. The man does not need to prove his social worth, but only that he is capable of caring for the woman.

Most important in the convention is that the reason for this dilemma often lies in the heroine herself. The new feminine qualities of independent thought and action are the very things that get the heroine into trouble. And she must be rescued from her dilemma by a man who is eminently qualified to resolve her problem, thereby proving, too, that he is eminently qualified to guide her through life—and further proving that she does not need independent thought and action if she has the right man for a husband. Margaret Deland gave the convention of the rescue from a dilemma full treatment in her novel *The Rising Tide* (1916). The heroine is twenty-five-

year-old Frederica Payton, a "new woman." Fred, as she is not
very subtly called, is in favor of birth control, women's suffrage
and labor reform. She smokes; she swears; she runs a rental
agency; she makes speeches to striking female workers; and
she has radical ideas about marriage. To old friend Arthur
Weston's comment that women should trust to chivalry, Fred
answers:

> "Thank you, I prefer to trust the ballot! 'Chivalry,' and women
> working twelve hours a day in laundries! "Chivalry,' and
> women cleaning spittoons in bear-saloons! "Chivalry,' and
> prostitution! No, sir! unless his personal interests are concerned,
> man's 'chivalry' is a pretty rotten reed for women to lean on!"[6]

Arthur is dismayed that she is so bold as to say it but must
admit the truth of what she says. When Fred talks about
marriage, there are obvious echoes of Margaret Fuller:

> "Of course, marriage generally hampers a woman. Perhaps
> because most of us are tied down to the old idea that it's got to be
> permanent,—which might be a dreadful bore! I suppose that's a
> hold-over from the time that we were chattels, and men taught us
> to feel that marriage was permanent—for us! They didn't bother
> much with permanence for themselves! But I admit that
> marriage—as men have made it, entirely for their own comfort
> and convenience, with its drudgery of looking after children—is
> stunting to women (p. 168).

Fred continues discussing her radical opinions and
scandalizes everyone in the novel. She gets into difficulty while
she is speaking to striking women at a rubber factory. A slight
disturbance breaks out. She tells a policeman "her opinion of
men in general and policemen in particular.... Fred punctuated
her remonstrances by putting an abrupt hand on his arm, and
instantly there was an unseemly scuffle" (p. 262). The result of
the scuffle is that Fred, her cousin Laura Maitland, and an
Italian worker all end up in jail. After some frantic phone calls,
Fred and Laura are rescued by Arthur Weston. Arthur takes
charge and arranges bail for them. He also promises to "patch
things up" so Fred and Laura won't have to go to court. Arthur
not only patches things up, he also persuades the press to
ignore the story of two society women in jail for fighting with
the police. He has quite effectively rescued Fred from the
possible results of her own folly.

The last element in the rescue pattern is that Fred must realize that Arthur is the man best fitted to guide her through life. He is already "the one person to whom she turned" in trouble (p. 276). When he tells her he loves her, she answers, "Well, I don't see any reason why I shouldn't marry you" (p. 285). This matter-of-fact answer is followed by, "You see we're friends; and you never bore me.... So—I will marry you, Arthur" (p. 286).

The rescue from jail helps Fred realize that she does not know everything, that a woman needs a man, and that faithful Arthur is perfectly suited to her. He is thoughtful, mature, and able to give her the guidance she needs. What the rescue from a dilemma taught Fred was that she could not effectively function outside the normal female role of dependence on a husband. Early in the novel, Arthur compares Fred to her cousin Laura:

> Laura was not so hideously truthful as Fred, and her conceit was not quite so obvious; yet she, too, was of the present—full of preposterous theories for reforming the universe! Her activities overflowed the narrow boundaries of domesticity, just as Fred's did; she went to the School of Design, and perpetrated smudgy charcoal-sketches; she had her committees, and her clubs, every other darned, tiresome thing that a tired man, coming home from business, shrinks from hearing discussed, as he would shrink from the noises of his shop or factory.... Yet Laura differed, somehow, from Fred; she was—he couldn't quite formulate it.... then the dim idea took shape: you could think of Laura and babies together, but a baby in Frederica's arms was an anomaly (pp. 38-39).

Fred's cousin, Laura Maitland, really embodies the limits that writers were willing to give to their heroines by World War I. Laura is intelligent and active but submissive to her husband. Her baby and husband remain the center of her existence. She tells Fred that "no woman really knew what life meant unless she had a baby" (p. 281). It is significant that Laura, too, must be rescued from jail because she was imprudent enough to be in a place where she was out of her natural role as wife and mother. In Laura's case, it was loyalty to Fred that put her into difficulty. Fred gets into trouble because she refuses to accept the traditional female position. She scoffs at Laura as a "slave" leading a "narrow" life (p. 276). But in spite of Fred's ideas about women's independence, when her activities get her into trouble, she must call for help—she must ask a man. The rescue from a dilemma does not lead Fred into love precisely, but it leads her to an awareness that Arthur is the man suited to her, the man she can depend on, the man who should be her husband. By the end of the novel, after the rescue, Fred is "snuggling" next to Arthur and planning for a family of her own. Having made the realization about her proper role, Fred shows no reluctance to enter it completely once the decision is made. She, in fact, convinces Arthur about the rightness of their union when he worries about the difference in their ages. Fred's extreme opinions have been at least somewhat eradicated by the rescue.

Another independent young lady is Patience Sparhawk in Gertrude Atherton's *Patience Sparhawk and Her Times.* Patience marries dashing, rich and very social Beverly Peele because of an intense physical attraction. Unfortunately, the attraction wears off, and there is nothing left in the marriage. Beverly is not Patience's equal in intellect, culture or sensitivity. "She persuaded herself that she loved him as much as she could love any man, and she did her pathetic best to shed some glimmer of spiritual light into a man who might have been compounded in a laboratory, so little soul was in him" (p. 213). The situation becomes unendurable, and Patience leaves her husband, a move which is necessary for her own happiness but which is also scandalous. She goes to work for a newspaper, causing more scandal.

When Beverly becomes ill, he persuades Patience to come back and nurse him, although she knows that she should not get involved with him again. She is overconfident of her ability to deal with the situation. At the same time, she is imprudent enough to express her hatred and contempt for her husband. When her father-in-law reminds her of her duty to her husband, Patience declares, "There is only one law for a woman to acknowledge, and that is her self-respect." To Beverly, she gasps, "Oh, how I hate you! I could kill you! I could kill you!" (p. 329). The two quarrel constantly over Patience's request for a divorce. When Beverly dies suddenly from an overdose of morphine, Patience is accused of his murder. She is sent to jail amid high public indignation against a woman who had left her husband and made shocking statements in the newspapers about women's rights. There is no doubt that Patience needs to be rescued:

> Her fine courage retreated, and mocked her. She had no wish to recall it. She longed passionately for the strong arm and the strong soul of a man. The independence and self-reliance which Circumstance had implanted, seemed to fade out of her; she was woman symbolised. No shipwrecked mariner was ever so desolate; for nothing in all life is so tragic as a woman forced to stand and do battle alone (p 394).

Her lawyer is Garan Bourke, a distinguished and brilliant attorney at the New York bar. Bourke struggles desperately to save her. By the time the trial ends, Bourke is no longer working for pay but for love:

> Is there any possible condition in which a man can appear to such supreme advantage as when pleading for the life of a fellow being, more particularly of a young and beautiful woman? How paltry all the time-worn rescues of woman from sinking ship and runaway horse and burning house. A great criminal lawyer standing before the jury box with a life in his hand has the unique opportunity to display all the best gifts ever bestowed upon man: genius, brain, passion, heart, soul, eloquence, a figure instinct with grace and virility.... She forgot her danger, forgot everything but the man.... As Burke finally dropped upon his chair, he turned to Patience. Their eyes met and lingered; and in that moment each passed into the other's keeping (pp. 445-46).

The jury votes guilty. There is a year of appeals which all fail. "I know, I know, that you will save me," Patience tells Bourke as she is taken to Sing Sing for execution (p. 454). The novel ends on a high moment of excitement. As Patience is being strapped into the electric chair, Bourke rushes in with the governor's stay of execution based on new evidence which Bourke managed to ferret out when everyone else had given up:

> Bourke had entered. He had followed the guard mechanically, neither hoping nor fearing until the far-reaching cheers sent the blood springing through his veins once more.
>
> He was neither clean nor picturesque, but Patience saw only his eyes. He walked forward rapidly, and lifting her in his arms carried her from the room.

THE END (p. 488)

The rescue ends the novel. Although the theme in much of the novel has seemed to be woman's independence, Patience has said that "however much she may reason, nothing can eradicate the strongest instinct in a woman—that she can find happiness only through some man" (p. 295). The problem the novel really deals with is the problem of a woman finding a man who is morally, physically, socially and intellectually suited to her. If she finds such a man, there is no need for independence. Garan Bourke is the man suited to Patience's needs. He has always been socially acceptable. The dramatic rescue here emphasizes that he has all the qualities she admires; he is the man who can handle all her problems.

In both Atherton's and Deland's novels, the independent young lady needs only the right man to be happy. The authors make it clear that the heroines are intelligent and perceptive and, therefore, an ordinary man will not do. But the rescue from a dilemma which has been created, at least in part, by the young woman's independent activities or opinions proves that there is a man who possesses the requisite intellectual strength and moral dependability. When that wisdom and dependability are present in the man, the need for the woman's independence diminishes rapidly. Both Atherton and Deland were consistently popular from the 1890s through the 1920s. As women writers, they seemed ready to explore the implications of some of the complaints of the feminists. As popular writers, however, they steadfastly delineated the basic belief of the public that bought the books—the best thing for a woman was a suitable marriage. The rescue convention offered a way to explore the problems and then resolve the issue of women's rights in a way to satisfy the readers' conceptions of proper feminine roles.

When the rescue from a dilemma appears in popular novels written by men, the heroine reflects some independent thought and action, but not the extreme positions shown by Fred and Patience. Initiative and drive, however, were beginning to be part of the popular heroine.

Southern writer George Washington Cable used the rescue from a dilemma in a novel with a heroine capable of shrewd analysis of her predicament and capable of making plans to help herself. In *The Grandissimes* (1880) the heroine is Aurora De Grapion, a beautiful, charming Creole widow. Aurora's problem stems from the fact that her late husband gambled away their plantation to Agricola Grandissime, who then killed him in a duel. Now Aurora and her daughter are living in straitened financial circumstances, unable to pay the rent, unable to buy much to eat. "Oh! Clotilde, my child, my child! the rent collector will be here Saturday and turn us out into the street!"[7]

Cable here makes it clear that Aurora's dilemma is not of her own making. She is a discerning and intelligent woman, but in this novel of Creole life, her possibilities for action are severely limited. Aurora pins her hopes on her ability to get a man to rescue her—specifically, she wants rich, powerful and attractive Honoré Grandissime (a relative of the man who killed her husband) to rescue her. Since the Creole society frowns on a lady accepting financial gifts from a man not connected to her, Aurora's task is to entice Honoré into marriage. She is already attracted to him, but she is clearheaded enough to know that his wealth and power add considerably to his suitability as her husband.

This novel is an example of the rescue from a dilemma. Cable differs from the later novelists in that, while he gives Aurora all the intellectual capacity and determination of the later heroines, he does not make her at all responsible for her dilemma. And, particularly interesting, Aurora knows before the rescue takes place that Honoré is the man suited to rescue her. Later novelists make the rescue of the heroine and her realization that she has met the right man for her occur at nearly the same time.

Aurora explains her position to her daughter:

> "My angel daughter," said Aurora, "if society has decreed that ladies must be ladies, then that is our first duty; our second is to live. Do you not see why it is that this practical world does not permit ladies to make a living? Because if they could, none of them would ever consent to be married. Ha! women talk about marrying for love; but society is too sharp to trust them, yet! It makes it *necessary* to marry. I will tell you the honest truth; some days when I get very, very hungry, and we have nothing but rice—all because we are ladies without male protectors—I think society could drive even me to marriage" (p. 255).

Aurora is concealing from her daughter the extent of her interest in Honoré, but the emphasis in this passage is clear, as well as stunning coming from the pen of a Southern gentleman. It is society's rule that ladies must be ladies, and they must be protected by men. If women could decide, many of them would prefer to make a living rather than marry. Although, within the boundaries of a novel about Creole society, Cable can allow Aurora very little independent action, he does allow her a great deal of independent thought. And it seems to be a measure of his respect for those sentiments that Aurora utters them without losing a shred of her natural feminine charm and appeal. In most later novels, the women who say such things are portrayed either as awkward creatures without feminine charm or as desperately and ineptly trying to enter a man's world for which they are totally unfit.

Aurora proceeds with her plan, and Honoré becomes more and more enamoured of her. The day comes when she receives a document giving her back the plantation and a credit of $105,000. The note from Honoré reads, "Not for love of woman, but in the name of justice and the fear of God" (p. 261). She has been rescued from poverty. And, most important, Honoré has rescued her for reasons of justice, not for reward. This kind of rescue proves that he is a man of strength and honor—a contrast to her first husband. Aurora now has money and so does not need Honoré for support. But Cable uses the rescue to show that marriage to the proper man is best. When Honoré proposes, Aurora tells him that she knows he will be the best man she has ever known and lets him "clasp her to his bosom" (p. 339).

Another heroine in a popular novel whose dilemma is not actually her fault is Mildred Jocelyn in *Without a Home* (E.P. Roe, 1881). Mildred's father is addicted to morphine, and, when his business fails, the family rapidly sinks from a life of affluence to one of impoverishment in the New York tenements. Mildred, trying to help support her parents and three younger children, takes a job as a clerk in a shop. The work exhausts her and wears down her health. Roger Atwood, a young man from the country determined to make a success by studying law, is in love with Mildred, but she rejects him as unrefined and uncultured. As the daughter of a morphine addict, Mildred's social level is hardly high, but she feels that Roger is beneath her in upbringing. Roger is aware that

Mildred thinks he is "coarse and rough," and "a country lout," but he vows to prove otherwise.[8]

In this novel, the young lady actively dislikes the man destined to rescue her. Contrary to the general pattern that places the rescue from a dilemma at the end of the novel, Roe puts it here in the middle of the novel because Roger must not only prove his dependability, competence and wisdom but he must also break down Mildred's resistance to him as a man.

Mildred's dilemma is increased when she is falsely accused of stealing and is arrested. As she is taken to jail, she looks back "hoping, for the first time in her life, that Roger Atwood was near.... She now did justice to his sturdy loyalty" (p. 341). In jail, she is so desperate that she vows, "If he can clear my name... if he will rescue my loved ones... I will make any sacrifice that he will ask. I will be his loyal wife" (p. 343). Roger tracks down the true story—another girl was the thief—and Mildred is freed.

Mildred's mother urges her to accept Roger. "Roger is not, and never will be, a weak man" (p. 372). Mildred is aware of Roger's sterling character; in fact, when he offers to send her father to a sanitarium, she is stunned. Now he is "the man who had saved her from prison and from shame—far more: the man who was ready to give all he had to rescue her fallen father" (p. 382).

But, in spite of her new appreciation of Roger and in spite of her gratitude, Mildred cannot feel real love for him; she cannot marry him. She continues to battle poverty alone. Most of her family dies; she is left with the two youngest children and must support them. She decides to study nursing. "I want a career," she tells her pastor (p. 487). Her dilemma—being alone in the world with responsibilities—continues, now partly from her stubbornness in not allowing herself to love Roger. But when Roger is hurt while stopping a runaway carriage and brought to her hospital, her resistance to him crumbles:

> "Roger... I am a weak, loving woman. I love you with my whole heart and soul, and if you should not recover, you will blot the sun out of my sky. I now know what you are to me. I knew it the moment I saw your unconscious face" (p. 519).

What is interesting in this novel is that Roger rescues Mildred from a dilemma to establish his dependability and strength, but he must also rescue someone from physical danger to excite her feminine emotions and wipe out her consciousness of the differences in their backgrounds. Roe apparently believed that a young woman would not be swayed to love by anything but a display of masculine muscle.

A novel with a plot completely structured around the rescue from a dilemma is James Oliver Curwood's *God's Country and the Woman* (1914). In the arctic north, six hundred miles from civilization, trapper Philip Weyman meets a beautiful girl dining alone in the wilderness. As if the meeting were not strange enough (she is using a tablecloth and serving canned lobster and boiled tongue), Josephine Adare immediately asks Philip to rescue her. "You would do a great deal for me? A great deal—and like—a man?"[9] When he assures her that he would, Josephine goes on, "And when you had done this, you would be willing to go away, to promise never to see me again, to ask no reward?" (p. 21). He promises to ask for no reward, although he is already inwardly assuring himself that she will be his if he helps her. She refuses to actually explain what her dilemma is. He must do what she tells him without knowing why:

> "I cannot tell you what my trouble is. You will never know.... If you fight for me, it must be in the dark. You will not know why you are doing the things I ask you to do.... Your one reward will be the knowledge that you have fought for a woman, and that you have saved her" (p. 33).

Since Philip is already in love with her (it took only two paragraphs), he agrees to ask no questions. Josephine wants him to return to her home and act as her husband. Her dilemma lies in her attempt to conceal the fact that her mother has given birth to a baby during her father's absence. Josephine is an independent, fearless young lady; she has concocted an elaborate plan to handle this problem; she deals forcefully with unsavory trappers and Indians; she conceals the truth from her father and directs her mother's actions. Certainly she is no fragile weakling. But she needs a man.

By the end of the novel, Philip has dealt with increasing complications, fought off renegades trying to blackmail Josephine, foiled her abduction, and burned the evidence against her mother. "Sweetheart, there is nothing more for me to know.... I will tell Father George that it has been your desire to have a second marriage ceremony performed by him.... Are you ready, dear?" (p. 346). Although Josephine has admitted earlier that she loves Philip, she has steadfastly insisted that she will not marry him. When her dilemma has been solved by this man who has done much more than she originally asked of him, she capitulates to the inevitable. "You may call him in, Philip. I guess—I've got to be—your wife" (p. 347). The curious tone she uses to agree to the marriage is probably meant to indicate not her reluctance, but her realization of the inevitability of that union.

Although Curwood was a writer of manly adventure stories, the rescue from a dilemma appears more often in domestic novels or novels about social issues. Harold Bell Wright includes the rescue from a dilemma in his first novel, *That Printer of Udell's* (1903), and in his extraordinarily successful *The Winning of Barbara Worth*. In both books, Wright uses the rescue to stress not only the capability of the man, but also his moral integrity in a world of uncertain moral values.

In *That Printer of Udell's*, Dick Falkner is not on either the same social level or the same moral level as Amy Goodrich, daughter of a prominent merchant:

> Dick's heart ached as he thought of his own life and the awful barrier between them; not the barrier of social position or wealth; that he knew, could be overcome; but the barrier he had builded himself, in the reckless, wasted years.[10]

Dick makes up for his wasted years by becoming a solid citizen, diligent worker, and active Christian. Unfortunately, as Dick's moral character improves, Amy's degenerates. She develops a love of frivolity. Finally, she quarrels with her father and defiantly runs away from home in the company of a man. When the man makes immoral advances, she leaves him; but now she is alone in the big city (Cleveland). She is friendless and starving, finally ending up in a brothel. Amy is in this desperate position because she cannot find work and cannot take care of herself in the city. She discovers her utter helplessness.

Dick has been searching all this time for her. On her first

night in the brothel (before she actually engages in any work), a Salvation Army group comes to sing in the lobby. Amy sees Dick in the group and faints. " 'O God!' the young soldier who had prayed last, sprang forward" (p. 379).

Dick takes her out of the brothel and arranges for her to live with a farm family while she rebuilds her shattered health and her shattered moral values. The question at this point is not whether Amy will accept Dick, but whether Dick can overlook Amy's moral fall:

> He was forced to confess, in his own heart, that he loved her yet, in spite of the fact that their positions were reversed; that he was an honored gentleman, respected and trusted by all, while she, in the eyes of the world, was a fallen woman with no friend but himself (p. 385).

The rescue proves that Amy needs guidance. She knows that she needs to be taken care of. "Won't you tell me what is best to do? I have thought and thought, but can get no farther than I am now" (p. 417). There is certainly nothing left of any independence now. Dick is the man to do her thinking for her. When he proposes, her response is tinged with relief. "Oh Dick, I do love you. Help me to be strong and true and worthy of your love. I—I—have no one in all the world but you" (p. 428).

In this novel, Wright uses the basic pattern of the rescue from a dilemma. Amy's dilemma comes at least partly from her willful actions and from her thinking that she could handle her own life. The dilemma is serious. Dick's rescue proves he has the moral strength to guide her through life and that he has the moral strength to overlook her sins. By the end of the novel, the relationship has been placed in the traditional pattern of male dominance and female submission.

In Wright's other novel, *The Winning of Barbara Worth*, Willard Holmes rescues Barbara's father from a dilemma. This twist to the pattern probably parallels the late nineteenth century variation in the pattern of the rescue from physical danger when the man rescues a male relative of the young lady to resolve ideological conflict. In this case, the ideological conflict is between Eastern capitalist exploitation and honest Western development. Willard, an engineer for the Eastern company that is only interested in squeezing profit out of Colorado, at first supports the company efforts to bilk

Jefferson Worth. But as he falls in love with Worth's daughter
Barbara, Willard realizes that he will need to show that he has
the Western attributes of honesty, strength and integrity and
that he has rejected the immoral capitalist goal of wealth at
any cost before he will be worthy of her.

When Worth is threatened with ruin if he cannot get the
payroll to his men, Willard joins Abe Lee in a desperate ride to
bring the payroll. They fight off an ambush, but Lee is
wounded and must stay behind in the desert while Willard
continues the desperate ride. Although he is rescuing Worth
from a dilemma, there is no doubt that Barbara is the focus of
the rescue effort: "The steady rhythm of his horse's feet seemed
to beat out the word: 'Barbara! Barbara! Barbara!' " (p. 416).
Willard arrives just in time to prevent a riot, "his face haggard
and drawn with pain," and slips off his horse at Barbara's feet
(p. 431). He has proved that he possesses the qualities deemed
important in the Western society of this novel and that he is a
proper match for the spunky Western heroine. "It is my desert
now; mine as well as yours," he tells her. "Oh, Barbara!
Barbara! I have learned the language of your land. Must I leave
it now? Won't you tell me to stay?" (p. 509).

Although Barbara herself does not get into a dilemma or
express radical ideas, she is representative of the new dynamic
heroine. Cawelti calls her "vigorous" with "purity and moral
worth" and "courage."[11] She does go to the engineering sites
with her father; she does live in primitive conditions amid
constant danger of riot, flood or some other natural disaster;
she does articulate the Western values. The man who wins her
must prove his ability to guide her life based on her values.

The rescue from a dilemma functions in all these novels as
a way to deal with the new independent heroine and the threat
that she represents to traditional roles. There is a measure of
relief expressed in the novels when the dilemma is resolved and
the heroine can fill the traditional role as a wife to a suitable,
respectable man. Since the popular heroine had begun to have
independent opinions and since she no longer screamed and
fainted at absolutely every crisis, the writers emphasized
qualities in the hero other than physical strength. That this
rescue convention is a way to conquer what appears to be a
threat to stability offered by the new heroine can be seen
through two major writers who use the rescue from a dilemma

specifically as a way to emphasize the inherent helplessness of woman regardless of any new opinions she might be expressing.

It is interesting that George Washington Cable, a Southerner, was able to allow his heroine some independent thought without downgrading her capacity as a woman. William Dean Howells, the Northern realist, presents a very dim view of woman's intellectual independence in *Dr. Breen's Practice* (1881). Dr. Grace Breen is a practicing physician, but Howells makes it clear that she does not have the true feminist radical philosophy. "She would not entertain the vanity that she was serving what is called the cause of women."[12] In an early discussion with her mother, Grace remarks, "A woman is reminded of her insufficiency to herself every hour of the day. And it's always a man that comes to her help" (p. 43). With this attitude, it is no wonder that Grace is shortly asking a male doctor to advise her about a case she doesn't know how to handle.

Dr. Rufus Mulbridge is intelligent, "incredibly gentle and soft... perfectly kind," and an excellent physician (p. 107). Grace's patient has a dangerous case of pneumonia, and Dr. Mulbridge pulls her through when Grace does not know what to do. In saving the patient, of course, he has saved Grace from her problem of being unable to handle the case. As a result of this rescue by Dr. Mulbridge, Grace decides to give up medicine because she feels inadequate for the profession. And, certainly, there is no more indecisive heroine in all fiction than Grace Breen as presented by Howells. At this point in the rescue convention, she should realize that Mulbridge is the man to guide her through life and perhaps help her in her work. In fact, when he proposes, he puts their relationship in those very terms. "I mean that I ask you to let me help you carry out your plan of life, and to save all you have done, and all you have hoped, from waste—as your husband" (p. 225). He explains: "You can't do anything by yourself, but we could do anything together" (p. 228).

Grace refuses his offer. She doesn't love him. She tells her mother that "The waste that I lament is the years I spent in working myself to an undertaking I was never fit for.... I like pleasure and I like dress; I like pretty things" (p. 234).

She promptly becomes engaged to Walter Libby, a nice

young man who owns several New England mills. "Oh," she tells him, "*nothing* is easy that men have to do!" (p. 249). Howells comments: "There are moments of extreme concession, of magnanimous admission, that come but once in a lifetime" (p. 249). Howells is using the convention of the rescue from a dilemma to create a rather devastating portrait of a woman trying to fill a man's job. Mulbridge here is offering the kind of marriage that a new woman ought to see as advantageous. But Grace opts for love and pretty things, just as, Howells implies, all women would. She needs to be rescued to realize her mistake in attempting to work in a man's field, but then she marries Walter, something that she could have done without any rescue situation if she had only had the sense not to stray out of her element in the first place.

Another elite writer who alters the pattern of the rescue from a dilemma is Henry James. In *The Bostonians* (1886), the dilemma that Verena Tarrent faces is the conflict between feminism and love. Added to the problem is the atmosphere of lesbianism that permeates the feminist movement in which Verena is the star speaker. Much of the novel deals with the struggle for Verena's affections between Olive Chanchellor, "unmarried by every implication of her being,"[13] and Basil Ransom, a "striking young man, with his superior beard, his sedentary shoulders, his expression of bright grimness and hard enthusiasm" (p. 5).

Verena's dilemma is that on the one hand she is crucial to the feminist movement and on the other, "she loved, she was in love—she felt it in every throb of her being" (p. 396). The larger dilemma that the reader sees is the struggle between natural and unnatural passions. Ransom is a Southerner with traditional views:

> He was addicted with the ladies to the old forms of address and of gallantry.... This boldness did not prevent him from thinking that women were essentially inferior to men, and infinitely tiresome.... He had the most definite notions about their place in nature, in society... (p. 197).

Olive wishes to devour Verena, to keep her from men such as Ransom:

> Olive wished more and more to extract some definite pledge from

> her; she could hardly say what it had best be as yet; she only felt
> that it must be something that would have an absolute sanctity
> for Verena and would bind them together for life (p. 113).

Verena's dilemma ends when Ransom arrives shortly before
she is to lecture and sweeps her away. But the novel ends with
James' ironic prediction:

> But though she was glad, he presently discovered that, beneath
> her hood, she was in tears. It is to be feared that with the union, so
> far from brilliant, into which she was about to enter, these were
> not the last she was destined to shed (p. 464).

James uses the pattern of the rescue from a dilemma but then
destroys the reader's confidence in the results. And Verena,
like Grace Breen, is swept away by love and acts finally in the
traditional female way, her feminist principles and the
importance of the movement slipping away. Howells presents
this reversion to traditional roles as good, but James, in this
novel about the feminist movement, seems to indicate that
there is peril in both the traditional and nontraditional roles.
Verena is not yet sufficiently independent to make reasoned
decisions about her life. She enters the feminist movement
because Olive dictates to her and exerts a powerful influence.
Then she yields to her feminine instincts, which are betraying
her into more misery.

It is probably not surprising that two male writers with
frankly feminist heroines are very hard on the value and
efficacy of the radical position. But the two female writers,
Atherton and Deland, with feminist heroines are equally hard
on the feminist principles. Deland is writing nearly thirty-five
years after Howells, and her view of feminine independence
remains much the same as his. The rescue from a dilemma in
all the novels, including those novels with less completely
feminist heroines, always proves that the woman needs male
protection and guidance. Since the rescue from physical
danger has been proving the inevitability of male dominance
since the beginning of the nineteenth century and since the
rescue from a dilemma continues to prove this inevitability,
even in the face of women's move for more independence and
intellectual respect, we must conclude that the traditional male
and female roles held an unchangeable value for the readers
throughout this long period.

One interesting point in the novels is that no one expects the rescue to take place more than the women themselves do. "Oh!" cries Grace Breen to Dr. Mulbridge, "surely you won't refuse to take the case!" (*Dr. Breen's Practice*, p. 102). When Verena is swept away by Basil Ransom at the moment she is to address a crowd of people, she tells her mother, "Mother, dearest, it's all for the best, I can't help it... let me go, let me go" (*The Bostonians*, p.461). When Fred is arrested, she immediately demands the right to telephone Arthur Weston. When Patience Sparhawk is arrested, she at once longs for "the strong arm and the strong soul of a man" (p. 394). Curwood's heroine, Josephine Adare, asks the first likely man she meets for help and says his reward will be that he aided a woman. Mildred Jocelyn hopes Roger Atwood will see her being led off to jail and come to her aid. When Amy Goodrich lapses into delirium, she calls for Dick to save her. And, of course, Cable's heroine, Aurora, plots from the beginning of the book to secure her own rescue.

This turning to men for rescue—it is presented as instinctual—effectively undercuts the image of women's independence and puts the heroine at once into the traditional female position. The rescue from a dilemma certainly appears to be a direct affirmation of the social value of marriage and the rightness of female submissiveness and male dominance. Dr. Mulbridge, the only man who offers marriage as a partnership for career and home, is rejected. In all the marriages, the man will be dominant. But these women who are entering a submissive position when they marry are still active, vital women. What do they do after they marry? There are not many specific answers in the novels, but we have a few hints. When Amy tearfully begs Dick to tell her what to do with her life, he advises her to do church work. "Write your father and tell him of your desire; that you cannot be content as a useless woman of society.... You will find many ways to be of use to others" (p. 418).

Grace Breen, who abandoned medicine in a wave of self-doubt, begins to volunteer her services to the children of her husband's mill hands. She does this work at her husband's suggestion: "She was not happy, indeed, in any of the aesthetic dissipations into which she had plunged, and it was doubtless from a shrewder knowledge of her nature that she had herself that her husband had proposed this active usefulness" (p. 270).

When Fred agrees to marry Arthur Weston, she says she doesn't think she could be like Laura and let her husband and children surround her. Arthur "smiled in spite of himself. 'Nature is a pretty big thing, Fred; when you hold your own child in your arms—,' he stopped short. 'Life is bigger than theories' " (p. 285). The activities the women seem destined to fill their lives with remain within the traditional bounds— charity work and domestic duties. It is probably also significant that the husbands have to suggest these activities. Just as they have to rescue the women from their dilemmas, so, too, they must advise them even in such standard feminine pursuits as charity work and domestic life.

Although the rescues in the novels affirm traditional marriage, the hero in the rescue from a dilemma is given some special qualities to make him worthy of the woman who possesses intellect, spirit and moral strength. The men in this rescue pattern, more than in the rescue from physical danger, offer established wealth and social position, absolute dependability and security from all of life's dangers. In addition, they appreciate the unique qualities of the women they are about to marry. It is not the woman's frailty that appeals to them, but the spirit that she demonstrates by trying (futilely, of course) to make her way independently. Arthur Weston very much admires Fred's honesty and intelligence. She never bores him. Both Patience Sparhawk and Mildred Jocelyn work very hard to earn a living, and both excite the admiration of men when they do so. The heroines in Cable's and Curwood's novels pit their wits against men and win. And it is Verena's magnetic presence while speaking that captivates Basil Ransom.

The heroes in Atherton's, Deland's and Curwood's novels are considerably older than the young women, a fact which adds to their images of stability and which emphasizes that the heroines need an experienced hand at the helm. All the men are successful. Garan Bourke is a distinguished lawyer; Arthur Weston, a respected trustee of large estates; and Philip Weyland has proved successful in the frozen north as a trapper. By the time Mildred realizes she loves Roger Atwood, he is a wealthy lawyer. Grace Breen does not marry the man who rescues her, but the man she does marry owns prosperous mills and takes her on a European tour as soon as they are wed. Honoré Grandissime is from one of the finest families in New Orleans and is very wealthy. Willard Holmes is an engineer with a wealthy background. Wright's other hero, Dick Falkner, has been elected to Congress as the novel ends. Only Basil Ransom lacks a base of stability and financial success—a lack which underscores James' ominous warning about Verena's future.

It is the hero's ability to handle the crisis that emphasizes his natural dominance over the heroine. However intelligent the heroine may be, it is the hero's skills and intellect that settle the problem. And again, as does the rescue from physical danger, the rescue from a dilemma shows the ideal view of male-female relationships: There is a man capable of caring for every woman; she has only to wait for him to appear. The rescue convention shows the idealistic belief that when a woman is in crisis, the right man will step forward to save her. If it is true that a man with all the proper qualities will appear, then clearly it is also true that there is no need for feminism.

When Patience Sparhawk says, "I refuse to admit that any human being has the right to control me," she adds at once, "When a man and woman are properly married, there is no question of authority or disobedience" (p. 327). Garan Bourke satisfies her imagination, "and he was the first man that ever had" (p. 414). These dynamic heroines need extraordinary men. But the rescue convention shows that these extraordinary men exist. The ideal marriage state requires complete affinity between man and woman—an affinity which is demonstrated by the rescue.

Marriage, believes Arthur Weston, is the "universal panacea" (*The Rising Tide*, p. 34). This statement in a novel aimed at women, written by a woman some seventy years after Margaret Fuller's document on feminism, seems to indicate rather decisively that, for readers of popular novels up to World War I, nothing much had really changed in what were desirable roles for men and women.

Chapter V

Woman Rescues Man

When a man rescues a woman in popular literature, whether from a physical danger or from a dilemma, the reward for his bravery or his wisdom is the woman he has just rescued—a prize. In fact, nearly all rescue situations provide the rescuer with some reward, tangible or intangible. Since the two major rescue conventions involving the male rescuing the female affirm traditional male dominance and female submission, a strong sense of divine inevitability pervades the novel's conclusion as the man and woman enter matrimony.

But what happens if the woman rescues the man? A quick answer is nothing very good. The popularity of the situation of the man rescuing the woman from either a physical danger or a dilemma would seem to indicate that a rescue pattern reversing the roles would simply add more useful plot variations to the patterns of the popular novel. Instead, however, the structure of the rescue when the woman aids the man becomes disjointed. The lack of structure probably reflects the uncertainty such a role reversal would cause in a society that stresses the values inherent in the convention of the man rescuing the woman.

The pattern of the rescue of a male by a female is consistent only when an Indian maiden saves a white man. When the rescuer is a white woman, the pattern for the convention becomes confused, and the purpose of the convention in the plot becomes vague. The convention no longer fits the plot of the novel in any effective way. This rescue pattern then, lacking a strong structure, fails to provide any sense of continuity in plot development or add any meaning to the novel's conclusion. Unlike the rescue of the woman by the man—which is integral to the overall plot and the conclusion—the rescue of a man by a woman is usually an odd insertion into the plot.

The convention then fails to substantiate the overall implicit value in all rescue conventions which is that there is reward in the present for good deeds. The woman who rescues a man generally gets no reward. Her action has no decisive effect on any possible marriage and reflects no sense of clear social value in the rescue effort. Since it does not support the overall ideal of sexual relationships expressed in the situations of the male rescuing the female, the rescue of a man by a woman flounders in trying to reflect any other ideal values.

In this rescue situation, a woman saves a man from threatening death or disaster. She acts bravely and decisively, just as a man does in the other rescue situations. But there the resemblance ends. The woman's display of bravery is not rewarded. It is often not much appreciated. Moreover, examples of a woman rescuing a man from a dilemma seem to be extremely rare, if they exist at all. That situation requires the rescuer to be wiser than the rescued party. Presumably, a woman in popular fiction may be as brave as a man, but she is never smarter than a man, so it would be impossible for her to rescue him from a dilemma. With these problems in structure and purpose, the convention of the rescue of a male by a female seems a waste of time, and one would expect that popular writers would never have attempted to use it. But the convention appears with some frequency during the period of this study. It is, however, often so loosely integrated into the plot of the novel, so uncertain in its purpose and so apparently lacking in social value that the very ambiguity in the convention may tell us something about the social attitudes of the readers.

The most clearcut pattern in this rescue convention appears when an Indian maiden rescues a white man. The source of this pattern lies in the myth of Pocahontas. Leslie Fiedler explains the myth of Pocahontas as one of four which formed a view of the West as a region where white American males fled to escape civilization:

> The first [myth] is The Myth of Love in the Woods or the story of Pocahontas and Captain John Smith, which presumably occurred in 1607.... Most Americans do not know the story, however, even in the version of 1624, but only as recast by the sentimental imagination of the early nineteenth century, to which period the myth, therefore, effectively belongs.[1]

Fiedler goes on to say that the Pocahontas legend appealed particularly to popular writers:

> The Pocahontas legend, despite its connection with the American West, is one which left untouched the imagination of our classical writers; it moved chiefly the producers of popular entertainment in prose and verse, between covers and on the stage, from the close of the eighteenth century to the verge of our own time.[2]

Pocahontas, as a character, has appeared in countless fictional narratives, and it is fairly obvious that most of the lovely daughters of Indian chiefs in American fiction derive directly from her image. But Pocahontas herself was rewarded for her actions. She was properly married to an Englishman and presented at the court of King James. The fictional pattern based on Pocahontas does not include a reward. The popular writers were faced with what Fiedler terms "the bugaboo of miscegenation" which terrified Americans.[3] The popular writers, then, had the peculiar writing problem of using the framework of a popular legend with a built-in rescue situation but being unable to conclude the situation in any satisfactory way because of a very strong social taboo against miscegenation. The answer most writers turned to was death for the Indian maiden.

Susanna Rowson, one of the earliest of American novelists, used the Indian maiden and the rescue in her 1798 novel *Reuben and Rachel or Tales of Old Times.* The plot of this rambling tale goes from the fifteenth century in Wales to the eighteenth century in America. Reuben Dudley (whose father was part Indian) has been raised and educated in England. Orphaned and poor, Reuben comes to America in search of the American estates that would be his inheritance. He is captured by Indians. While a captive, he is asked to teach white culture to the lovely Eumea, the daughter of the chief.

The teaching activity goes on for five months until the Indians decide to kill Reuben. Eumea warns him. "Englishman, awake, get up; death and danger are at hand."[4] She spirits him out of the camp. Once past the guards, she "threw her arms around the neck of Reuben, bathed his cheek with her tears, pressed her cold trembling lips to his, and sobbing Adieu! returned to her restless bed to weep and pray for his safety" (II, p. 347). Reuben flees through the woods but falls ill of a fever. Fortunately for him, Eumea was unable to control her emotions and has followed him. "Is it strange that I should follow you;... was it possible that Eumea could stay behind you and live.... I will follow you, my dear instructor, I will be your handmaid, and love and serve you to the last hour of my life" (II, p. 347).

She nurses him through his illness and leads him to safety. Eumea has saved the man from certain death. When they reach civilization, Reuben locates his inheritance and promptly weds Jessy Oliver, an English girl. Understandably, Eumea is upset. Looking wild and in a broken voice, she tells him, "Eumea will rest no more, know peace no more. I had raised a deity of my own, built an altar in my bosom, and daily offered the sacrifice of a fond, an affectionate heart.... Farewell, do not quite forget the poor, poor Eumea" (II, p. 360). She then drowns herself in the pond. Although Reuben does have Indian ancestry, he never entertains any romantic thoughts toward Eumea. Here, the miscegenation taboo seems somewhat linked to the degree of civilization the Indian may have. Reuben is, for all practical purposes, an Englishman. Eumea is a savage. In spite of her dying plea, Reuben probably will forget her immediately. The episode, while it possesses some sentimental appeal, has no significance in the plot of the novel.

Another Indian maiden driven to suicide appears in E.D.E.N. Southworth's *The Three Beauties, or Shannondale* (1851). Southworth was a lady who knew what the public wanted. As late as 1930, Street & Smith had ninety of her books in print.[5] This novel was a domestic tale set in the Shenandoah Valley. It is a mark of how appealing the Pocahontas legend must have been that Southworth, finding no practical way to get an Indian into her plot, inserted an episode in which an old priest tells the legend of Lover's Leap. In this tale, Englishman Colonel Clinton is thrown by his horse while on a fox hunt. He lands in a forked tree projecting out the side of a precipice. He is rescued from this dangerous position by the fabulously beautiful Indian queen Lulu. "Her form was tall and majestic, but beautifully proportioned. A small, but regal head.... Her eyes were large and dark, full of liquid fire, fierce and soft..."[6] The beautiful Lulu rescues Colonel Clinton, sets his broken arm and nurses him back to health. She also falls madly in love. "She left her Indian crown; she left her glorious heritage of independence, of love, of worship, and of power, and followed like a slave the footsteps of her chosen master" (p. 30). Of course Clinton tires of Lulu. On the day of his marriage to another, Lulu sings her death song, jumps off the cliff and drowns. The only reason Southworth could have had to include this story was that the tale of an Indian maiden rescuing a white man was so popular that including it automatically enhanced the novel's appeal whether or not it enhanced the novel's coherent structure.

The Indian maidens do not seem to be able to judge the quality of the men they fall in love with. Malaeska, the heroine of the first dime novel, *Malaeska; The Indian Wife of the White Hunter*, is married to William Danforth, whom we first meet as he is flirting with a white girl. Later, William's comment to Malaeska about his son reveals his lack of feeling for his Indian family. "It's a pity the little fellow is not quite white" (p. 33). However, when Danforth is being chased by Indians, he is very glad that Malaeska is there to hide him and convince his pursuers that he is not at home.

She saves his life—and is rejected immediately. Since William is being hunted and must leave the territory, she assumes that she will go with him. But William "had never thought of introducing her as his wife among the whites" (p. 38). His pride and his fear of "scorn," "disgrace," and "degradation" cause him to leave her behind. Malaeska bows her head in submission and accepts his decision. She remains faithful in her devotion to this man. Later, when she finds him dying after an Indian skirmish, she comforts him and looks forward to joining him in the great hunting grounds. Malaeska's story continues through painful trials and tribulations. She is rejected by her son when he is young. And, years later as a grown man, he kills himself on learning that she is his mother and that he has Indian blood. Malaeska dies stretched over her son's grave. Stephens calls her "the heartbroken victim of an unnatural marriage" (p. 251). And certainly, Malaeska's whole story is about the awful consequences of marrying outside one's race.

Catherine Sedgwick, sometimes called the first domestic novelist,[7] used the Indian maiden in her novel *Hope Leslie or Early Times in The Massachusetts* (1827). In this novel, fifteen-year-old Magawisca is working in the Fletcher household as a servant. Indians attack, led by her father the chief, and capture the fourteen-year-old Everell Fletcher. In true Pocahontas fashion, Magawisca comes to the rescue just as Everell is about to be chopped up by her father. As the chief raises his blade, Magawisca "screamed 'Forbear!' and interposed her arm."[8] The blow severs her arm. "Stand back!" she cries, "I have bought his life with my own. Fly, Everell—fly" (I, p. 136). He escapes to England.

Seven years pass and Everill returns to America. He does remember Magawisca and tells his servant, "Yes, Digby, I might have loved her—might have forgotten that Nature had put barriers between us" (II, p. 52). The barriers, which are endlessly discussed in this novel, are race, religion and culture. Magawisca has never been willing to convert to Christianity; she is always referred to as a savage. Everell's remark about the possibility of love is probably more sentimental than realistic. In any case, now he is in love with his cousin Hope Leslie.

Everell does repay his rescue when Magawisca is seized and thrown in jail for being a witch. Everell and Hope contrive a disguise which enables her to sneak out of prison. Magawisca slips away in a boat, clutching a locket containing a lock of Everell's hair. Magawisca fares better than most Indian maidens since she is alive, even if maimed, and has some satisfaction in the fact that Everell repaid her rescue by rescuing her in turn. Few other Indian maids had that satisfaction.

Two novels by popular writers of masculine adventure stories imply that the Indian maid's true reward came when she died to preserve the man's life. Jack London's novel *Smoke Bellew* (1912) is set in the Klondike. The hero, Smoke Bellew, is prospecting when he and his partner Shorty are taken captive by some Indians led by a white man named Snass. Of course, Snass has a lovely daughter, Labiskwee, whose mother was French, English and Indian. Labiskwee thinks of herself as English and tells Smoke over and over that she is white. "I am English and I will never marry an Indian—would you?"[9] She is soon in love with him. "I love. We are white, you and I" (p. 348). Labiskwee takes Smoke's love for granted, and he does not correct her since she is his only means of freedom.

Shorty escapes, but Smoke is watched too closely to get out

of camp. Happy in her love, Labiskwee still realizes that Smoke wants to go back to the white world. Because she loves him, she rescues him. "I have thought much. The hunger for the world would come upon you, and in the long nights it would devour your heart" (p. 358).

She makes a cache of supplies outside camp and sneaks him past the guards. Then she leads him on the dangerous trail west. Unfortunately, they get lost, and after a month their food runs out. "Smoke and Labiskwee knew their danger. They were lost in the high mountains and they had seen no game" (p. 364). They survive the "white death" because Labiskwee knows they must cover up with furs until the dangerous mist passes. They struggle west without food. Finally, Labiskwee is lying in a stupor, helpless. She is dying. With her last bit of strength, she puts a pouch in Smoke's hand. When he opens it, he finds a "tiny flood of food" (p. 380). She has saved her rations for him. He eats and gets enough strength back to continue on to safety. Labiskwee literally starved herself to rescue him.

A similar situation takes place in Stewart Edward White's *The Silent Places* (1904). White wrote some fifty books—all masculine adventure stories. In this one, Dick Herron and old Sam Bolton are sent out by the Hudson Bay Company to track down and bring in for punishment an Indian who has not paid for his outfit. Before they leave, Dick notices a lovely Indian maiden in the tribe which is trading at the post. Dick pays her some compliments, which mean little to him but which cause May-may-gwán to fall desperately in love with him. When the two men set out on their journey, she trails after them. Dick is furious. "She'd hinder us, and bother us, and get in our way, and we'd have to feed her—we may have to starve ourselves— and she's no damn use to us. She can't go. I won't have it."[10]

The men try threats and pleading, but she will not turn back. She pathetically trails after them, stumbling through the woods, over streams and up mountains. She helps with chores but gets no gratitude from Dick. When Dick breaks his leg, May-may-gwán faithfully cares for him and tends the camp alone for three months while Sam goes off to hunt for food. Without May-may-gwán, the men might not have been able to survive. Sam is grateful, but Dick is not. He remains "profoundly indifferent to the girl" (p. 167). He is really more than indifferent; he is hostile.

May-may-gwan's major rescue effort comes when Dick and Sam have lost the trail of the renegade and have no idea which way to go. Everything seems hopeless. But May-may-gwan goes off with a passing Indian and sleeps with him so he will tell her which way the renegade has gone. When she finds out what the white men need to know, she kills the Indian to cover their trail. Her efforts save them from returning to Hudson Bay post in defeat and also help them establish their own position in the frozen north. Although Sam is grateful, Dick still ignores her. She tells Sam that it is enough "that I am near him... that I can raise my eyes and see him breaking trail" (p. 222).

Finally, in the territory known as the Barren Grounds, they are out of food and starving. Sam is too weak to go on. If they cannot find the renegade in the next day, they will have to give up and try to make it back to the post. Dick pushes blindly forward with the one remaining dog. May-may-gwan totters after him. He beats her; she still follows. He kills a fox and shares it with the dog, ignoring the starving girl; she still follows him. When she collapses in the snow, he leaves her. But a belated attack of conscience sends him back.

Poor May-may-gwan thinks that his return means he loves her. "Oh Jibiwanisi, I am yours, yours, yours! You are mine. Tell me" (p. 284). 'I am yours,' Dick lied steadily; 'my heart is yours, I love you' " (p. 285). She dies happy, promising to wait for him at the border of the "next land." At that moment, the renegade staggers up, snowblind. So the delay occasioned by the Indian maiden's death keeps Dick in the right spot long enough to capture the renegade. He manages to get Sam back to the post, and they are rewarded for their valiant effort. May-may-gwan, who secured their success with her sacrifice, is dead. One more sacrificial Indian maiden—one more unrewarded rescue.

Even a devotee of the Pocahontas legend should be appalled by the truly pathetic story of this girl's devotion and the insensitive treatment she receives from the man she loves. White, however, was extremely popular; the book was a bestseller. So we must assume that the story of the Indian maiden's rescue effort and sacrifice remained as appealing in 1904 as it had been in Rowson's story of 1798.

A book by Basil King (*The Wild Olive*, 1910) contains an

exception to the very rigid pattern of the convention when an Indian maiden is rescuing a white man. In King's novel, Norrie Ford, a fugitive from a death sentence (he is innocent, of course), is fleeing through the Adirondacks when a beautiful girl appears in the woods and beckons to him. She leads him to a remote cabin where she brings him food and conceals him from the posse prowling the area. She refuses to tell him her name or much about herself. He does, however, see "the hint of dark eyes flashing with an eager, non-Caucasian brightness—eyes that drew their fire from a source alien to that of any Aryan race."[11] The beautiful girl does tell him at last that she is the daughter of a Virginian and the wife of a French Canadian. "I believe," she says, "she had a strain of Indian blood" (p. 43). The girl is illegitimate, but her father provided handsomely for her before he died, and now she is very wealthy. Her guardian is Judge Wayne—the man who sentenced Norrie to death.

When the girl decides that the time has come for Norrie to move on, she leads him through the woods to Lake Champlain. She has hidden a boat there filled with provisions. She provides luggage, a ticket on a steamer for Ireland, and a wallet filled with money. She has worked out a route for him to take to Canada, and, furthermore, she provides him with a false identity. She has not only saved him from death but she has given him ample means to start a new life. Norrie is grateful but does remark several times that she is not his type of girl.

Years pass. Norrie travels to Argentina and makes a success in business there. He also becomes engaged to lovely Evelyn Colfax, the niece of his boss. King tells us that all this while the girl Miriam Strange was waiting for Norrie to return. "If he never came, she would rather go on waiting for him— uselessly! Her heart was listening for a call" (pp. 163-64). Miriam and Norrie finally meet again at a society dinner party in New York. Coincidentally, Miriam is an old friend of Evelyn's. When Miriam tries to tell Norrie that nineteen-year-old Evelyn is too young for him (he is thirty-two), he thinks she wants "payment of a long standing debt" (p. 191). Miriam is horrified that he thinks so. She insists that her fears for his marriage are based on Evelyn's immaturity. When Norrie reveals his past and starts an attempt to clear himself, Evelyn sticks by him at first but then can't stand the strain and breaks the engagement. In the meantime, Miriam rescues Norrie again when she agrees to marry a long-time admirer, Charles Conquest, a brilliant lawyer who promises to defend Norrie if Miriam will marry him. At the end of the novel, when Norrie has been cleared of the old murder charge, he realizes that he loves Miriam. "You'd be committing a sacrilege against yourself—if you married anyone else but me" (p. 326). Conquest, when told the whole story, releases Miriam, and she and Norrie are free to wed.

Miriam is the only Indian woman to be rewarded with the love of the man she rescues. The setting in this novel is not on the frontier, but in the drawing rooms of New York. The time is contemporary. Miriam is Indian only in her ancestry not in her culture. She has money, and King has presented her character as intelligent, morally strong, and respected by everyone. She is definitely not a savage. A jaded reader might wonder if this remarkable woman is getting much of a reward in Norrie, but the readers who put this novel on the bestseller lists of 1910 were not such cynics.

When the rescue convention used an Indian maiden rescuing a white man, readers must have known what to expect. But when a white woman did the rescuing, the convention became less consistent. It was used in a few novels where the hero is socially beneath the heroine. In these cases, the heroine has started out showing very undemocratic feelings about the man's social position. If the heroine is overly conscious of her own social superiority, the reader begins to wonder if she is worthy of the stalwart hero. No matter how important social status may have been, the ideal of social mobility remains rooted in democratic principles, and heroines were not supposed to exhibit undemocratic values.

In Mary Johnston's *To Have and To Hold*, Jocelyn Leigh is being rescued by Ralph Percy, who has married her to protect her from Lord Carnal. Since Jocelyn insists on a marriage in name only and since Ralph must fight off Lord Carnal several times and defy the direct orders of the king, the reader begins to wonder if Jocelyn is worth all this effort. When Ralph is arrested on a charge of piracy and brought before the Virginia governor on trial, Jocelyn proves her worth by rescuing him.

She asks permission to speak and makes an eloquent plea for his release. "A pirate! [We were] prisoner to the pirates, and out of that danger he plucked safety for us all" (p. 257). To convince the governor, Jocelyn asks Lord Carnal to tell the truth about the incident. He agrees—if she will kiss him. Jocelyn loathes the man, but she makes the sacrifice for Ralph. Ralph is cleared, and the governor apologizes. "Captain Percy, I beg to apologize to you for words that were never meant for a brave and gallant gentleman" (p. 260). Jocelyn's sacrificial gesture to save Ralph convinces the reader that she is indeed worthy of this brave man. Even more important, the rescue proves that she loves him.

The Princess Mary, in Charles Major's *When Knighthood Was in Flower*, must convince the reader that she is worthy of Charles Brandon after she fails to rescue him from the Tower. After Brandon's rescue of Mary, he is clapped into the Tower by King Henry on two charges of murder. Since Brandon killed the man in defense of Mary, she has a clear moral obligation to save him. But Mary is a spoiled princess, who doesn't want the king to know that she was out the night Brandon rescued her. So the reader waits in suspense and Brandon waits in the dungeon while Mary procrastinates. Finally, a loyal friend negotiates Brandon's release. Mary is now in the position, as far as the reader is concerned, of being superior to Brandon socially and inferior to him morally.

She and Brandon elope, but they are intercepted; Brandon goes back to the Tower. This time Mary proves she has a conscience. She pleads with the king, her brother. "Take my life and spare him—spare him!" (p. 296). The sacrifice Henry demands is that she marry aging Louis XII of France. She agrees and so rescues Brandon from the Tower. Now the reader knows that Mary's moral strength is worthy of Brandon, who has risked everything for his love. After Louis dies, Mary and Brandon can marry.

Another lady who must prove her inner worth is Molly Stark Wood, heroine of Owen Wister's *The Virginian*. Molly is descended from one of the finest New England families. "Had she so wished, she could have belonged to any number of those patriotic societies of which our American ears have grown accustomed to hear so much" (p. 90). Molly's character has been formed by pride. Although she seems to love the Virginian, she feels that he is beneath her and is too conscious of their different educational and social backgrounds to accept him. She is planning to leave Wyoming when, during a ride, she finds the Virginian wounded by Indians. Molly tries desperately to revive him and get him back to safety:

> She tore strips from her dress and soaked them, keeping them cold and wet upon both openings of his wound.... She built another fire.... Meanwhile, she returned to nurse his head and wound.... Then she poured her brandy in the steaming cup, and, made rough by her desperate helplessness, forced some between his lips and teeth.... "Listen, friend," said she. "Nobody shall get you, and nobody shall get me" (pp. 327-29).

She does rescue him. During his convalescence, she realizes how much she loves him. The rescue proves to the reader that Molly is not as heartless as she has seemed and that she does love the Virginian. Her inner worth is greater than her pride.

These three women are proving their moral worth to the reader, not to the hero. The hero is already in love. But until the moment when the woman rescues the hero, the reader has not been certain that she possesses the good character such a man deserves. The women in these novels are also repaying their own earlier rescues by these men.

Another young lady who repays her own rescue is Ray Longstreth in Zane Grey's *The Lone Star Ranger*. Ray had been saved by Buck Duane from a robber's attack. Buck is working under cover for the Texas Rangers, investigating Ray's father, Colonel Longstreth. One night, he is trapped when the Colonel returns unexpectedly to his study. Buck dashes through the house to Ray's room. She conceals him. "They might shoot you before you got away. Stay. If we hear them, you can hide. I'll turn out the light. I'll meet them at the door. You can trust me" (p. 296). When her father knocks at the door, Ray tells him she is going to bed, saving Buck from detection.

Ray's rescue of Buck not only repays her own rescue but also proves that she does not have the criminal inclinations of her father. She has begun to suspect that her father is a criminal, and in concealing Buck, she chooses the morally right position.

These young ladies all marry the men they rescue—but not as a result of that rescue. When the male rescues the female from physical danger or a dilemma, the rescue provides the impetus to a romance, culminating in marriage. The young woman and her family begin to appreciate the man's superior character, and he is in a position to prove that he is capable of caring for the woman he rescued, that he is the right man for her. The rescue by the female does not work in these ways. The four men rescued in the situations just described are already in love with the women. If there are doubts about the worth of the women, they belong to the reader. Since a woman is never required to be the man's support, there is nothing further to prove there, and no sense of inevitability attends the rescue event. The purpose of the rescue convention here is only to establish the woman's moral character for the reader.

In other novels where the writer uses the convention of the female rescuing the male, the purpose is less clear. Melissa, the mountain girl in John Fox's *The Little Shepherd of Kingdom Come*, rescues Chad twice—once at the beginning of the novel when they are both youngsters in school and once at the end of the novel when they are grown up. In the first episode, Chad is being bullied at school because he is a stranger. Melissa comes to his aid. "You wouldn' dare tech him if one of my brothers was here, an' don't you dare tech him again, Tad Dillon" (p. 39). Her eye "spoke with the fierce authority of the Turner clan and its dominant power for half a century," and the bullies slink away. Chad is grateful although he is too embarrassed to say so. On the way home, he wishes a wild-cat would leap into the road so he could fight it and save her.

The second time Melissa rescues Chad is during the Civil War while Chad is with the Union forces. Melissa in the mountains hears that a rebel guerilla is planning to ambush and kill him. During a raging storm, she makes her way down the mountains to Chad's camp to warn him. But she slips away before he can return with the sentry to thank her. As a result of being out in the rain, Melissa gets pneumonia. She did not expect to be rewarded for her rescue because she has always known that Chad can never be hers. Melissa is illegitimate. For a while, Chad thought that he too was illegitimate, but he knew that the question of his birth was not as difficult for him as the question of her birth was for Melissa:

> It came with a shock to Chad one day to realize how little was the tragedy of his life in comparison with the tragedy in hers, and to

> learn that the little girl with swift vision had already reached that
> truth and with sweet unselfishness had reconciled herself. He was
> a boy—he could go out in the world and conquer it, while her life
> was as rigid and straight before her as though it ran between close
> walls of rock as steep and sheer as the cliff across the river (p. 155).

Melissa can gain nothing from her rescues of Chad. Her stigma of illegitimacy bars her future as effectively as their race bars the Indian maidens.

Fox may have included Melissa's rescue effort in his novel for sentimental effect. There seems to be no clear reason for George Barr McCutcheon to use the rescue convention in *Jane Cable* (1906). The hero Graydon Bansemer enlists in the army and goes to the Philippines during the Spanish-American War. While there, he becomes the protector of beautiful refugee Teresa Velasquez. When he is wounded, his love, Jane Cable a volunteer nurse, cares for him. Teresa describes to Jane how she saved Graydon's life while he was grappling with a Filipino. "I seized a pistol that was lying near me and fired; the Filipino fell."[12] Teresa says that she loves Graydon, but because he loves Jane, she is leaving. This rescue situation is only a brief episode in the plot. We do not even see the rescue; Teresa describes it to Jane in a few sentences. The rescue episode really serves no structural purpose in McCutcheon's novel.

The purpose of the rescue of a man by a woman in James McHenry's *The Betrothed of Wyoming* seems to be only a warning that a woman should not rescue a man. Isabella Austin is in love with ruthless Tory John Butler. When he is imprisoned, she deceives the jailer and rescues Butler. Butler, however, shows neither gratitude nor love toward his rescuer. Isabella took a grave risk at the time of the rescue, but her risk is far reaching. The other characters feel sorry for her. Butler ignores her. Finally, Isabella goes insane. She is accidentally killed during a battle—a pathetic mad figure—a woman scorned. The young lovers in this novel are Henry Austin and Agnes Watson whose romance began when Henry rescued Agnes from an Indian attack. Isabella's failure to win love with a rescue while her brother Henry does win love with a rescue probably shows the root of the issue: it is not natural for women to rescue; it *is* natural for men to rescue.

This lack of naturalness made the convention awkward to

handle. Just how awkward it could be is evident in the ridiculous plot of Oliver Wendell Holmes' *A Mortal Antipathy* (1885). In trying to set up the rescue situation as plausible, Holmes introduces the heroine, eighteen-year-old Euthymia Tower, as a dynamo of feminine strength:

> While all her contours and all her movements betrayed a fine muscular development, there was no lack of proportion, and her finely shaped hands and feet showed that her organization was one of those carefully finished masterpieces of nature....[13]

Euthymia handles dumbbells "too heavy for most of the girls" (p. 41). She also performs daring feats on the trapeze and rows on the crew of her college.

The hero of this novel is Maurice Kirkwood who has a special problem. When he was two years old, Maurice was accidentally tossed over a balcony by his lovely seventeen-year-old cousin. The result of this accident is that Maurice has an extreme antipathy to lovely young women. If he is in the presence of a young woman, he has a seizure and faints. Holmes speculates that a rescue by a young woman will counteract the accident caused by a young woman, and Maurice will be cured of his antipathy. In order to set up this situation, Holmes has forced his heroine and hero to switch traditional sexual qualities. The result is that the reader feels disjointed; his expectations are askew. It is difficult to see Maurice as a hero at all.

Maurice gets typhoid fever. While he is recovering, his house catches on fire. He is too weak to flee the flames. "He tried to call for help, but his voice failed him, and died away in a whisper..... he sank back upon the pillow, helpless" (p. 264). Of course, Euthymia dashes into the burning house to rescue him. She picks Maurice up and carries him out "as easily as if he had been a babe" (p. 274). And as Holmes predicted, Maurice is cured of his antipathy. "You must not leave me," he tells Euthymia. "You must never leave me. You saved my life. But you have done more than that..." (p. 282).

It is easy to see why this novel never made the bestseller list. Aside from other ludicrous aspects in structure and development, the hero and heroine do not reflect any of the reader's common expectations for such characters. And while Euthymia has a certain attractive quality in her healthy animal strength, Maurice, in his helplessness, has no appeal at all. The novel is useful here to show the difficulties writers faced in trying to set up a rescue of the man by the female. The rescue from physical danger with inverted sexual roles not only lacks appeal, but also lacks verisimilitude. The difficulty lay in the writers not being able to fit the situation into the novel's structure so that it was integral in the overall plot and so that it reflected the value system of the novel and that of the readers who would buy the book. The writers who used the convention with the Pocahontas myth had the advantage of using a situation that readers expected to be a passing episode in the life of the hero, not crucial to his future domestic happiness.

The cultural importance of the traditional sexual roles is clear in a novel in which the young lady tries but *fails* in her rescue effort. Robert Montgomery Bird introduces the lovers in *The Hawks of Hawk-Hollow* (1835) when Catherine Loring tries to rescue Hyland Gilbert. Hyland falls out of a tree into the river rushing over a fall. Catherine "did not pause.... she ran down to the rocks that led to the base of the fall and rushed into the water."[14] She grips the body, but he is too heavy and she can't pull him to safety. Fortunately, at that moment a passing stranger jumps in and rescues Hyland.

Catherine fails in her rescue effort, but she, in fact, wins in a way that few of the other women do. Hyland falls in love with her at once. He responds just as the women do when the men succeed in rescuing them. "So heroic!" he says, "instead of committing me to my destiny, with a pathetic scream, to run at once to my assistance, like an angel, rather than a woman!" (I, p. 135). Catherine's heart is right, but her strength is inadequate. She, therefore, fills the proper female role. Hyland adores her. "Such an admirable creature! so gentle, and yet so firm! so frank, yet so modest! so merry, yet so dignified" (I, p. 153). It is simply not woman's role to rescue successfully. In failing, Catherine has proved her womanly qualities, and Hyland loves her for those qualities.

To emphasize doubly the principle being expressed here, Bird sets up a physical rescue for Hyland at the end of the novel. Hyland rescues Catherine from a forced marriage when he interrupts the ceremony in a dramatic fashion and carries her away:

... a young man... rushed into the circle and displayed to the eyes of
the bride the features of the younger Gilbert. She uttered a
scream... crying with tones as wild and imploring as his own,
"Oh,... save me!" and fell into a swoon (II, p. 64).

The implications in the way Bird used both the convention of
the female rescuing the male and the convention of the male
rescuing the female from physical danger are clear. In failing
to rescue, Catherine proves her womanliness. In rescuing,
Hyland proves his masculinity. The traditional roles of the two
lovers are maintained. The reader is in familiar territory.

The social values reflected in the convention of the female
rescuing the male are revealed as much in the awkwardness
with which writers used it as in any effectiveness it may have
had. As Fiedler said, it is obvious that, appealing as the myth
of Pocahontas was, writers could not reward these women with
the love of the men they rescued. The rescue situation in
general cannot elevate someone above his race and its level in
the society. The rescue could not elevate Cooper's Uncas
sufficiently to allow him to marry Cora Munro, and it cannot
elevate these Indian maidens enough to wed the white men
they rescue—even though, like Cooper's Uncas, the maidens
are Indian royalty. The only Indian woman to succeed in the
way we might expect is Miriam Strange in *The Wild Olive*. And
Miriam as a character has virtually nothing in common with
the other Indian women.

Of the seven Indian women, one is a queen and four are the
daughters of chiefs. Considering the good matrimonial
possibilities such young women would have, it is difficult to see
exactly what appeal these young men had for them. Five of the
seven are indifferent or even cruel to the women. The
implication seems to be that any white man is more desirable
as a mate than an Indian. And having once loved a white man,
the Indian maiden is unable to accept an "inferior" Indian.

Malaeska demonstrates this concept when she refuses to
wed a chief. She has returned to her tribe after her son has been
taken away by his white grandfather. Her husband is dead,
and she is alone. The women of the tribe wish to kill her, but she
is saved by a chief. The chief had once loved her and now
proposes again. "Malaeska, my wigwam is empty; will you go
back?" (p. 140). She refuses because she expects to meet the
husband who deserted her in the happy hunting grounds.

Instead of marrying a chief and beginning a new life, Malaeska lives a lonely isolated existence on the edge of white civilization until she dies. And it is noteworthy that Stephens ignored the reward pattern in the chief's rescue of Malaeska to make this point of lifelong devotion to the faithless white man.

None of the Indian maidens is allowed to do the practical thing—shrug off rejection by the ungrateful clod she rescued, find some likely brave, and produce several strapping children. The Indian maidens in the novels of Rowson and Southworth commit suicide when they are rejected. Stephens' heroine pines away. Sedgwick's heroine sails off to a lonely future. When London and White kill off their Indian maidens, they make the women happy to die so that the unworthy objects of their affection can live. White, in fact, stresses May-may-gwan's happiness as she dies hearing Dick say his first kind word to her—a lie.

The two primary social attitudes that seem to be paramount in the rescue of a white man by an Indian maiden are an absolute belief in white supremacy and an appreciation of complete female submission. The figure of the Indian maiden rescuing and serving the white man she loves shows both concepts in bold relief. The sensitivity of the reader of today may be horrified by the picture of May-may-gwan tottering through the snow after the man who ignores her, but obviously, the readers of 1904 did not react that way.

It is easy, too, to sympathize with Melissa in Fox's novel, but she dies as surely as the Indian maidens die. Melissa is illegitimate and would bring the man down socially just as the Indians would. Clearly, a man is not expected to give up any social status for love. These women have the insurmountable barriers of race or birth—romance is not possible.

The situation of the female rescuing the male does reflect some positive democratic values. Although it is good to be a member of the upper class in these novels, it is not acceptable to be too proud of it. The heroines in the novels of Johnston, Major and Wister are too proud. They need to show that they have the right moral instincts and that they truly love the men who have already rescued them. The rescue convention is useful for showing that the woman is capable of an unselfish act and is not really tied to undemocratic views of social levels.

Perhaps the most important social attitude reflected in this rescue convention is that women must not be too obvious in expressing their love. The Indian maidens are very frank in their affections. May-may-gwan may seem like an extreme case, but the others are equally intense in their devotion. Southworth's Lulu gives up her queen's crown to follow Colonel Clinton, and Rowson's Eumea follows Reuben away from her tribe. None of these maidens is asked to come—each unabashedly follows, pleading for love and affection, offering to serve until she dies.

London's heroine is leading Smoke Bellew to safety, but she is equally obvious in her affections. "Her glances were love glances; every look was a caress" (p. 349). Sedgwick's Magawisca adores Everell. "She had done and suffered much for him, and she felt that his worth must be the sole requital for her sufferings" (II, p. 126). When she sails off, she takes a lock of his hair. Malaeska accepts insult and desertion in "humble submission" and remains loyal to her worthless husband (p. 38).

But it is not only the Indian maidens who display their love too conspicuously. The mountain girl Melissa in Fox's novel is devoted to Chad from childhood on. When Chad thinks of the two girls in his life, he thinks "Melissa was the glow-worm that, when darkness came, would be a watch-fire at his feet— Margaret, the star to which his eyes were lifted day and night" (p. 152). Unlike Melissa, Margaret does not reveal her love for Chad until he first reveals his. When Melissa is dead, Mother Turner tells Chad that Melissa had "fought his battles so fiercely that no one dared attack him in her hearing" (p. 334). The dead girl has preserved his footprint in the mud outside the cabin door, and she died with his name on her lips. Unlike most of the men, Chad feels guilty about not returning Melissa's love. He decides not to go back at once to Margaret in the valley. He "would send Margaret word, and she would understand" (p. 336).

Chad's appreciation of Melissa's emotions is rather exceptional. Most of the men ignore the woman's love or else deliberately reject her. McHenry's Isabella Austin is driven to madness by Butler's rejection and his pursuit of other women. She has no appeal for him once she displays her love. And Teresa Velasquez gives up her love for Graydon saying, "Dios, how I loved him! I would have gone through my whole life with him!" (*Jane Cable*, p. 256).

Six women do marry the men they rescue. Of those six, the Princess Mary (*When Knighthood Was in Flower*), Jocelyn Leigh (*To Have and To Hold*), Molly Stark Wood (*The Virginian*), and Ray Longstreth (*The Lone Star Ranger*) all know before the rescue takes place that the men love them. Although the reader knows Miriam Strange loves Norrie Ford, Miriam never reveals her affection to Norrie until he first acknowledges his love (*The Wild Olive*). Holmes' heroine, Euthymia, does not meet Maurice until she rescues him, but he had already noticed her—although he could not speak to her because of his antipathy. The social value in these rescues is clear. Men must pursue, and women must wait. And the woman who does not wait loses her appeal.

Women are not rewarded for rescuing men the way men are rewarded for rescuing women. The female rescue does not excite the interest of the male, establish the woman as an appropriate mate, or create a sense of inevitability about the union. The fact that eight of the fifteen women die probably means that the writers, unable to reward them, could only envision death as the next logical step. Indeed, since in the ideal state there is one man for every woman, there is little else to do but die when one's love is not returned.

The rescue effort itself, accompanied by obviously displayed affections, totally demolishes the traditional values of women—weakness, shyness, modesty and helplessness. The rescue then displays none of the qualities that make a woman appealing. Therefore, the ideal of relationships between the sexes is expressed only in the male rescue of the female. The ambiguous use of the rescue convention as applying to women rescuing men shows that the popular writers could find no consistent way to use the situation to structurally reinforce the social values in the novels. What the rescue of the male by the female does seem to prove overwhelmingly is that she shouldn't have done it.

Chapter VI

The Ideal of the Rescue

The rescue convention in popular novels written before World War I always produced excitement and tension. Fiction is littered with rescues from both the dreadful dangers and the petty annoyances of life. The four rescue patterns examined here, however, not only produce excitement and interest but also embody the main elements of the system of social values held by the reading public before World War I. In *The Popular Book*, James D. Hart insisted that the popular writers were those who understood the public's beliefs and were able to incorporate those beliefs into fiction:

> Literary taste is not an isolated phenomenon.... Books flourish when they answer a need and die when they do not.... There are many books whose popularity relates to a most subtle blending of appeals to ...needs of the public. Yet, in some way or another, the popular author is always the one who expresses the people's minds and paraphrases what they consider their private feelings.[1]

Hart felt that the result was "a dynamic interplay of reader, writer, and the times in which both lived."[2] The value of the rescue convention for us lies in what it reflects about those readers, writers and times.

All the rescue patterns embody two major ideals: good actions and rewards. The rescue situation shows that good exists and that it is an active force. The result is reward to the good person who has acted. Although none of the rescuers asks for reward —it is a criterion of goodness that the deed is done for its own sake—all the rescuers get rewarded. The sole exception to this ideal is the woman who rescues a man in a potentially romantic situation. In this exception lie social values that are obviously so crucial that they override the ideal that is present in all other rescue patterns. The reward for most of the rescuers, however, is in the present. This ideal state of good actions and reward in the present reflects the world as the readers wanted to believe it existed.

Beyond the ideal state, the four rescue patterns show social values which have varying degrees of importance. The most important social value seems to be rooted in the consciousness of class that filters through all the rescue patterns and the attendant plot situations.

The rescue itself presents moral worth in action, unattached to any considerations of birth or class. The democratic ideal of the self-made man, the rise from obscurity on merit, and the equal possibilities for all who have a decent start in life are all, apparently, the basis for the rescue convention. Yet we see that this democratic ideal is the gloss that covers the rescue pattern. The democratic ideal works well in the rescue of a child. The orphan develops into an exemplary citizen when rescued and given a fair start in the world. Although most of the children are orphans when they are rescued, they do come from varying backgrounds. Patience Sparhawk's mother was a promiscuous drunkard. Barbara Worth's parents were wealthy Easterners. Little Gertrude in *The Lamplighter* has been abandoned in the street. Young Ben Blair sees his mother die while his drunken father berates her. Chad Buford in *The Little Shepherd of Kingdom Come* is a sturdy young mountaineer trying to make his own way. The range of background implied in these examples is important in the overall value being expressed by the rescue of a child. No matter the background, the child, once rescued, is brought up in an atmosphere that nurtures the best qualities he possesses. And the respect and success he attains in adulthood come entirely from his own achievements and merits.

But when marriage enters the picture, the democratic ideal of individual merit begins to weaken. Although the man's rescue of the woman from physical danger opens the doors to a rise in social status, the rescue effort and the man's subsequent success cannot fully overcome a low or questionable birth. Marriage is simply too intimate a connection. The popular writers fell back on the convention of the revelation of upper class birth or true identity in order to avoid actually allowing a lower class character to marry an upper class character. It seems obvious that, while readers supported the democratic principle of individual worth, when it came to marriage, they wanted the traditional reassurance of good birth. Fox's *The Little Shepherd of Kingdom Come* shows this split in the ideal.

The orphan Chad attains a high degree of respect and admiration based on his own attributes of courage, integrity, intelligence, moral character and honesty. But when Chad falls in love with the plantation owner's daughter, Fox has to clear up the question of his birth before the romance can continue.

The act of rescue cannot elevate the young man far enough to wed the rich young lady. The consciousness of social class is heightened when the potential romantic situation involves someone who is not white. Blacks and Orientals do not usually appear as major characters in the novels. So the race question centers on the Indian. The American Indian, as noble savage, presented fictional possibilities for excitement and pathos that popular writers could not overlook. But when the noble Indian appears in a rescue situation with romantic possibilities, there are problems. Since most Indians are in novels with frontier settings, the race question is compounded by the problem of radically different cultures. No matter how noble, the savage remains a savage. The Indian maidens have the double handicap of being savage and of failing to comply with traditional female reticence. They are punished on both counts. The fact that death for the Indian was most often chosen by the writer as the solution to the romantic problem may well reflect the final answer to the Indian problem that was being acted out in nineteenth-century America.

The issue of religious differences between the man and the woman usually does not appear. In some cases, the man or woman must give up godless ways and accept the path of Christianity before the marriage can take place. St. Elmo has to give up his life of dissipation before Edna Earl will marry him. Christine Ludolph must accept God before she is worthy of Dennis Fleet (*Barriers Burned Away*). But the romantic problem of the Christian and the Jew or the Protestant and the Catholic was not a situation popular writers were interested in. The absence of such a problem in the romantic plots probably means that for the public it was unthinkable that such a problem would arise.

The popular novelists saw no difficulty in matches with foreigners—the foreigners were always titled. The novels firmly support the value of a definite social hierarchy. The relief expressed when birth or identity was revealed shows how pressing an issue social class was when linked with marriage. No one is more relieved than Beverly when the goatherder she has agreed to marry turns out to be Prince Dantan (*Beverly of Graustark*). For Americans before World War I, the democratic ideals mingled strangely with a traditional belief in the values of social class. When marriage was involved, class became the deciding factor.

The second important reflection of social values comes in the traditional sexual roles, supported strongly in these popular novels. The rescue patterns in which the reward is present are the man's rescue of the female from physical danger or from a dilemma. The overwhelming value expressed in these patterns is that man must be dominant and woman must be submissive. These roles will lead to happiness. A violation of these roles, as when the woman acts aggressively and reveals her love (when she rescues a man), will lead to unhappiness. In the rescue from a dilemma, even the most feminist heroines realize the rightness of the traditional roles. When Patience Sparhawk is in deep trouble, she yearns for "the strong arm and the strong soul of a man" (p. 394). Every woman in popular fiction longs for a strong man to guide her, and every man looks for a helpless woman he can protect and care for. The late nineteenth-century novels with independent heroines allowed some exploration of woman's position, but the rescue pattern cleared the way for the solid social value of male dominance and female submission. The man's reward for rescue was the woman. The woman who rescued got no reward. The message is plain.

The two rescue patterns in which men rescue women also reveal attitudes about age and accomplishment. The rescue of a female from physical danger always is performed by a young man. The rescue from a dilemma usually is handled by an older man. There are obvious practical considerations in this division. It is not as easy for a forty-five-year-old to stop a runaway carriage as for a twenty-year-old. But the implication in this division is in what society expects at a certain age. The rescue from physical danger generally opens the way to romance. What the man must do next is start his upward climb to financial success. He has used his brute strength; now he must use his head. But the rescue from a dilemma relies on wisdom and stability in the rescuer. This man is at an age when society expects that he has developed these qualities. He no longer needs brute strength.

These two men symbolize the process of success. A man begins to make his way in the world through his natural physical strength, and he is regarded as successful when he can handle his affairs with his brains. Only the writers of male adventure stories continued to stress physical strength in the older man.

The degree of possible financial success was considerable. Men worked their way up to wealth and professional positions. They did not settle for mediocre jobs and modest income. The men who rescued women from dilemmas were usually quite wealthy. The ideal state lay in great wealth and a powerful position.

It is noteworthy, too, that although the older man is considered a candidate for romance, there are few older women in the romantic arena. A man's value increases with age and mounting financial success. A woman's value fades with age. All the May-December unions are presented as advantageous to both parties. The young woman gets substantial security. The older man gets renewed vigor in his empty life. The social attitude toward marriage, then, was that marriage was an exchange. In spite of all the romantic trappings that might attend the event, the men brought financial security and the women provided beauty and charm.

The consciousness of class and the consciousness of correct male and female roles are the two paramount social values shown in these rescue patterns. There are, however, several other social values distinctively presented. One is the value of hard work. The rescued children work hard when they grow up. In the rescue from physical danger, the young man works hard to prove that he can support the young woman he has already proved he can protect.

Hard work is a positive value to the society. It is also a positive value to the person working. In these novels, hard work brings success. No one toils hopelessly—unless he has terrible moral lapses that drag him down. The rescue situation provides the opportunity, and the hard work brings the success. A good moral life will support the person through hard times or hard work. While Dennis Fleet toils night and day to get ahead, he staunchly resists the allure of alcohol (*Barriers*

Burned Away).

Along with hard work, education is a definite value. One of the major benefits the orphan receives when he is rescued is the chance for a good education. Although Huck Finn may not have appreciated the values implicit in education, the other orphans did. A great part of the future success is based on the education that opened the doors. The young ladies who become renowned authors all have to have the educational opportunities necessary to expand their perceptions of the world. Edna Earl spends most of her time studying in the library and emerges as a religious scholar of international repute (*St. Elmo*). It was through education that the American ideal of the self-made man could be reached.

Other definite social values lay in service to the community. Men were expected to serve their country. Most heroes either were just out of the military, were about to enter the military, or had been in the military for a time. Along with military service, heroes were expected to fight corruption in business. This corruption was a social problem that gained attention in fiction after the Civil War. Wright's novel *The Winning of Barbara Worth* concentrates on corruption as represented by Eastern capitalists. The hero must reject and fight these forces before he is worthy of the heroine.

And in all the rescuers and all the children who are rescued is manifested the attribute of courage. The act of rescue, with its accompanying risks, requires courage. Even more, the future activities of these characters require courage—physical and moral. Chad Buford joins the Union Army because of his moral convictions (*The Little Shepherd of Kingdom Come*). When he becomes a lawyer, Ishmael Worth refuses to take a case if his client is not truly innocent.

The rescue itself brings out the finest qualities of mankind. The fictional patterns in the novels supported a network of social values that gave substance and purpose to the readers' lives. The value of past popular literature lies in its ability to give us a window to the past so that we can see those values of daily life as well as the hopes and dreams of people in another time. John Cawelti bases his belief in the importance of popular fiction on those very grounds:

It may be that, when he most powerfully embodies the thoughts

and feelings unique to a particular period, the artist is, at the same
time, creating something that, by virtue of its special relation to its
own times, cannot attain more than an ephemeral place in the
history of culture. The ability to express the spirit of the moment
may not be as important an artistic characteristic as the appeal to
universal human concerns in a lasting way; nonetheless, I have
come to believe... that this is a distinctive kind of artistry worth
studying in its own right.[3]

Leslie Fiedler, discussing the bestselling epic of the nineteenth
century, *Song of Hiawatha,* warns that "a nation which
expurgates from its anthologies those great bad poems it has
loved... is a nation with only half a memory."[4]

The popular novel shows us the spirit of the moment. And
it is apparent that the rescue convention is a major component
in those novels. The rescue could be used to express both the
ideal values and the actual values of the times. For these
reasons alone, the rescue convention would be prominent.

But the rescue convention offered something more. It
expressed an ideal state even beyond the factors of good action
and reward. The rescue expresses an ideal of intense
desirability—the ideal that the possibility of rescue exists. No
matter the danger or dilemma, we can be rescued. What's more,
we *will* be rescued.

In Simms' *The Yemassee* Pastor Matthews shouts "God be
praised!" when Harrison rescues Bess (p. 344). Many prayers
and thanks were directed to God when rescues took place. But
the reason the rescue was so satisfying as a convention was
that it was performed by human beings. The rescue was that
splendid overthrowing of a seemingly omnipotent fate—a new
chance—a glorious possibility.

For the readers the ideal world contained rescue, rescue
from both the awful crises and the numbing "quiet
desperation" of life. That "damned mob of scribbling women"
and all the other popular writers knew what readers wanted—
they wanted to be rescued.

Appendix

The following are plot synopses of the popular novels used in this study.

Alcott, Louisia May. *Rose in Bloom.* 1876.

Rose Campbell, now twenty, is back from her European tour and preparing to take her place as heiress to a fortune. Rose has a philanthropic nature and does much charity work. Her first love is her cousin Charlie, but he is beginning to drink too much at parties. Charlie is killed in a fall from a horse. Rose continues her philanthropic work and adopts an orphan brought to her by her cousin Mac. Eventually Rose and Mac grow to love each other and marry.

Atherton, Gertrude. *Patience Sparhawk and Her Times.* 1895.

Young Patience Sparhawk is taken in by elderly Mr. Foord after her drunken mother dies in a fire. Patience is sent to San Francisco and lives with Miss Tremont, a temperance leader. Eventually Patience meets rich, dashing Beverly Peele. There is an intense physical attraction between the two, and they marry. The marriage is a mistake, and Patience leaves her husband to become a newspaper reporter. Beverly becomes ill, and Patience returns to nurse him, while pleading for a divorce. When he dies from an overdose of morphine, she is accused of his murder. Garan Bourke, a brilliant lawyer, defends Patience and falls in love with her. She is convicted and sentenced to die, but Bourke rescues her at the last moment when he uncovers fresh evidence.

Bacheller, Irving. *Eben Holden.* 1900.

Eben Holden, an itinerent farm worker, takes care of young orphaned Willie. They settle at the farm of David Brower, and Willie grows up to marry Hope Brower and work on the New York *Tribune.* Later Willie goes into politics. Eben lives to a peaceful old age and dies.

117

Bennett, Emerson. *The Forest Rose; A Tale of the Frontier.* 1850.

In the Ohio River valley in 1789 Albert Maywood loves Rose Forester. Rose is captured by Indians. Albert and trapper Lewis Wetzel pursue and rescue her. Unfortunately, the Indians recapture her, and Albert must rescue her again before they can wed.

Bird, Robert Montgomery. *The Hawks of Hawk-Hollow.* 1835.

In Delaware during Revolutionary War times, the members of the Gilbert family, once feared and hated by neighbors, are reported to be dead. The family estate is owned now by Colonel Falconer, an old enemy of the Gilberts. The youngest Gilbert, disguised as a painter, returns to the territory and falls in love with Catherine Loring after she tries unsuccessfully to rescue him when he falls into the river. After much political maneuvering—Hyland is a patriot, unlike his Tory family—Hyland rescues Catherine from a forced marriage. All ends well when Hyland is revealed to be the son of Colonel Falconer.

Cable, George Washington. *The Grandissimes.* 1880.

There has been a long family feud between the aristocratic Creole families the Grandissimes and the De Grapions. Lovely widow Aurora De Grapion is living in poverty in New Orleans with her daughter Clotilde because her husband lost their plantation gambling with old Agricola Grandissime and then was killed in a duel. She carries on a calculated plot to win the love of Honoré Grandissime. He returns the plantation to her for the sake of justice and then reveals his love. They wed and the feud ends.

Cooke, John Esten. *The Virginia Comedians or Old Days in the Old Dominion.* 1854.

Aristocrat Champ Effingham becomes enamoured of actress Beatrice Hallam. She rejects him, but he continues his lustful pursuit. In the meantime Beatrice is rescued from drowning by Charles Waters, who is revealed to be her cousin. Beatrice and Charles fall in love, but Champ continues his pursuit. Finally, Champ kidnaps Beatrice and Charles rescues her although he is wounded by Champ, who flees to Europe. Charles and Beatrice wed and live happily. Champ finally returns from Europe, a reformed man.

Cooper, James Fenimore. *The Last of the Mohicans.* 1826.

Hawkeye and his Indian companions, Chingachgook and Uncas, escort the sisters Alice and Cora Munro to Fort William Henry to join their father. The villainous Huron Magua lusts after Cora and pursues them. After being captured and then rescued, the girls arrive at the fort. Unfortunately, they are captured again during the massacre of Fort William Henry. Hawkeye, the Indians, and Duncan Heyward, Alice's betrothed, manage to rescue Alice, but, according to Indian law, Cora remains Magua's prisoner. Uncas leads a last desperate rescue attempt, but both he and Cora are killed.

Cummins, Maria,*The Lamplighter.* 1854.

Eight-year-old orphan Gertrude is taken in by Trueman Flint, the kindly lamplighter. After he dies, she goes to live with rich Miss Graham. She grows up to love her childhood playmate, Willie Sullivan. While visiting Saratoga, Gertrude fears that Willie loves Isabel Clinton. In a boat disaster, Gertrude nobly rescues her supposed rival from the burning boat. She later finds out that Willie still loves her. She also discovers her long lost father, now a rich merchant.

Curwood, James Oliver. *God's Country and the Woman.* 1914.

In the frozen arctic, trapper Philip Weyman meets beautiful Josephine Adare who asks him to help her. She wants him to pose as her husband so that she can convince her father that she is married and has a child. Actually, she is trying to conceal the fact that the child is her mother's. Philip agrees and masquerades as Josephine's husband. He foils an attempt to blackmail the women, and destroys the evidence against Josephine's mother. The child dies. Phillip and Josephine wed when everything is settled.

Deland, Margaret. *The Rising Tide.* 1916.

Frederica Payton is a young woman who believes in all the feminist positions and supports women's suffrage. She is active in that cause and in labor disputes. Demonstrating her belief in equality, she proposes to Howard Maitland, but he rejects her. He admires her but loves her more conventional cousin Laura. Fred's confidence in the feminist belief in equality is shaken. It is shaken further when she is arrested and thrown into jail for fighting with the police during a labor strike. Old friend Arthur Weston gets her out of jail, and Fred realizes that he will make the best husband for her. She further realizes that her feminist positions are too extreme and must be modified.

Fox, John Jr. *The Little Shepherd of Kingdom Come.* 1903.
　　Orphan Chad Buford is taken in by the Turner family in the Kentucky mountains. On a trip to Lexington, he gets lost and meets Major Buford who takes him in and provides him with an education. They discover that Chad is really the descendant of a relative of the major's. Chad loves Margaret Dean, but they are estranged when he joins the Union Army during the Civil War. After the war, they reconcile. On a visit to the mountains, Chad finds that Melissa, also adopted by the Turners, has died as a result of the pneumonia she got while warning him about an ambush. Melissa's evident love for him disturbs Chad, and he decides to forego his own happiness for a while and head west to start a new future.

Garland, Hamlin. *A Little Norsk or Ol' Pap's Flaxen.* 1892.
　　Settlers Bert Gearheart and Anson Wood take in a five-year-old orphan they name Flaxen. The girl grows up happily with the bachelors. When she is fifteen, she marries a boy from town and leaves them. Bert has fallen in love with her and heads west after the marriage. Flaxen has a child but grows to hate her worthless husband. When her husband leaves town because of debts, Anson comes to stay with Flaxen, and they are a happy family with Anson acting as grandfather. Bert returns when Flaxen's husband dies, and he and Flaxen wed.

Grey, Zane. *The Lone Star Ranger.* 1914.
　　Buck Duane kills a man in a fight and becomes a fugitive. He joins an outlaw camp when he meets a girl who has been forced to stay there and work. Buck and Jennie escape, but they are tracked down, and Jennie is killed. His failure to rescue

Jennie haunts Buck, and he agrees to work under cover for the Texas Rangers in exchange for a pardon. He begins to investigate Colonel Longstreth, major of outlaw-infested Fairdale. He falls in love with Longstreth's daughter, Ray, and she saves him from detection. When Longstreth is at last exposed as corrupt, Buck and Ray wed and go to Louisiana to build a new life.

Holland, Josiah G. *Sevenoaks; a Story of Today.* 1875.

Robert Belcher is a corrupt mill owner in a New England town. He has stolen the proceeds of several inventions of Paul Benedict and driven him and his small son Harry to the poorhouse. Trapper Jim Fenton rescues both Harry and his father. Benedict eventually recovers his healthy mind. Belcher continues his ruthless business practices until he is exposed by Mrs. Dillingham, a social dilettante who is the sister of Benedict.

Holman, Jessee L. *The Prisoners of Niagara or Errors of Education.* 1810.

As a baby, William Evermont is rescued from Indians by a trapper who gives him his name. Growing up with a farm family, William is miserable and asks a passing gentleman to be his father. The gentleman agrees, and William goes to live with Major Hayland, after first rescuing the major's niece, Zerelda, from the Potomac River. William grows up and is educated, but he becomes sexually promiscuous when he is fifteen and wastes his time in sexual escapades. Finally, he settles down and joins the Indian fighters. After rescuing Zerelda from Indians, William discovers he is the son of Sir William Valindon. He and Zerelda marry.

Holmes, Oliver Wendell. *A Mortal Antipathy.* 1885.

Maurice Kirkwood comes to live in Arrowhead Village, a New England town. The townspeople do not understand why the young man does not mingle with the young ladies. Maurice gets typhoid and tells the doctor treating him that he has an antipathy to young women because his female cousin dropped him over a balcony when he was a baby. Holmes speculates at length whether such antipathy could be cured by a young woman who saved Maurice instead of injuring him. When a fire in his home breaks out, Maurice is rescued by Euthymia Tower, a strong, athletic young lady. Maurice loses his antipathy, and he and Euthymia wed.

Howells, William Dean. *Dr. Breen's Practice.* 1881.

Dr. Grace Breen becomes a physician because she is disappointed in love. Now, as a young doctor, she discovers that she is completely inadequate as a physician. She must get the assistance of Dr. Rufus Mulbridge to save her first patient. Grace decides to quit medicine and rejects Mulbridge's offer of marriage and a joint practice. She decides women should not try to do men's work. She marries Walter Libby, who is rich and can give her pretty things.

Howells, William Dean. *Indian Summer.* 1886.

Theodore Colville, an American publisher, goes to Florence for a vacation and becomes engaged to Imogene Graham, who is twenty years his junior. Imogene is staying with Evalina Bowen, a widow with a young daughter. Colville worries about being older than Imogene, but he decides it doesn't matter. While on a carriage ride, Imogene refuses to jump into Colville's arms when the carriage teeters on the brink of a precipice. She realizes at that moment that she does not love Colville, and she breaks the engagement. Colville subsequently realizes that he loves Evalina Bowen, who has been waiting patiently for him to reach that decision.

James, Henry. *The Bostonians.* 1886.

Olive Chancellor, a radical feminist, hears lovely Verena Tarrant speak and realizes that the young woman has a gift for swaying audiences. She enlists Verena in the feminist cause and takes her into her own home, urging her to promise that she will never marry. Olive's cousin, Basil Ransom, who has come to Boston from Mississippi, becomes enamoured of Verena and courts her. There is open hostility between Basil and Olive as each struggles for control over Verena. On a night Verena is to speak, Basil appears and sweeps her away, out of the feminist cause and into marriage.

Johnston, Mary. *To Have and To Hold.* 1900.

Ralph Percy, a Jamestown settler, meets a young lady who

has just arrived on a bride ship. Jocelyn Leigh, the king's ward, has fled to America to escape marriage to Lord Carnal. Ralph marries Jocelyn to protect her. Lord Carnal arrives in Jamestown and continues his pursuit of Jocelyn. When a message arrives from the king ordering Jocelyn back to court and Ralph to face arrest, the couple flee. They run into pirates, but Ralph manages to take command of the band. When he refuses to fire on a British ship, the pirates mutiny, and Ralph and Jocelyn are picked up by the British. Ralph is on trial facing charges of piracy when Jocelyn eloquently pleads for his life and saves him. Lord Carnal is maimed by a panther and commits suicide. Ralph and Jocelyn are free to return to England with the king's pardon.

King, Basil. *The Wild Olive.* 1910.

Norrie Ford is a fugitive in the Adirondacks, having escaped jail waiting execution on a murder charge. He meets a beautiful girl who hides him in a cabin, feeds him and arranges for his escape to Canada. She refuses to reveal her name, so he calls her the Wild Olive. Ford eventually reaches Argentina where he becomes successful in business and falls in love with lovely, young Evelyn Colfax. On a business trip to New York, he meets Miriam Strange at a party and realizes that she is the Wild Olive. Miriam is a friend of Evelyn's and tries to tell Norrie that his proposed marriage is a mistake. In an effort to clear himself of the old murder charge, Ford reveals his true identity. Miriam promises to marry an admirer, attorney Charles Conquest, if he will defend Ford. Conquest does clear Ford, but Evelyn becomes hysterical and breaks the engagement when Ford must return to jail for a time. Ford then realizes that he really loves Miriam. Conquest releases Miriam, and she and Ford can wed.

Lillibridge, William Otis. *Ben Blair, The Story of a Plainsman.* 1905.

Wealthy rancher Rankin takes in orphan Ben Blair after his drunken father disappears and his mother dies. Twelve years pass. Ben is a young man and in love with neighbor Florence Baker. Florence decides to move to New York with her mother so that she can meet eligible men of the upper social class. Rankin is killed one night by a rustler who turns out to be

Tom Blair, Ben's father. Ben hunts his father down and takes him to jail where Ben is wounded while stopping a lynch mob. He discovers evidence that he is really Rankin's son, but he destroys it because the dead man had not wanted it known. Ben goes to New York, and Florence realizes she loves him.

London, Jack. *Smoke Bellew*. 1912.

Smoke Bellew quits his job as an editor on a San Francisco newspaper and heads for the Klondike for adventure. He has many brushes with death and takes up prospecting. While on the trail with a partner, Smoke is captured by a band of Indians led by a white man named Snass. Smoke's partner manages to escape, but Smoke is too closely guarded. Snass has a daughter, Labiskwee, who falls in love with Smoke and helps him escape. They travel west to freedom, but their food runs out, and they grow weak. As Labiskwee dies from starvation, she gives Smoke her food ration that she had saved for him. The food gives him enough strength to reach safety.

McCutcheon, George Barr. *Beverly of Graustark*. 1904.

Beverly Calhoun is the daughter of a Southern senator. She decides to visit her friend, Princess Yetive of Graustark. While she is traveling through the hills to reach the kingdom, her drivers desert, and her coach is seized by mountain bandits. The bandit leader is Baldos, a goatherder. Baldos saves her from an attacking mountain lion, and Beverly feels he possesses nobility beyond his lowly station in life. She finally reaches the capital of Graustark to find there is war with evil Prince Gabriel of Dawsbergen. There is much political turmoil before Prince Gabriel is overthrown and Baldos reveals he is really Prince Dantan, the rightful ruler of Dawsbergen. Although Beverly had already agreed to marry him, she is thrilled that Baldos has turned out to be a prince.

McCutcheon, George Barr. *Jane Cable*. 1906.

Jane Cable is the daughter of railroad tycoon David Cable. Cable's wife never told her husband that she had adopted the girl while he was out West. James Bansemer, an unscrupulous lawyer, arranged the adoption. Now Jane is in love with Graydon Bansemer, the lawyer's son. Bansemer has been involved in numerous shady dealings over the years, and he is now under heavy pressure. Because Jane's mother has refused his advances, the lawyer reveals Jane's adoption in public. Graydon still wants to marry Jan, but she refuses since they do not know her parentage. Finally, while in jail, Bansemer reveals her upper-class birth, and Jane and Graydon wed.

MacGrath, Harold. *The Adventures of Kathlyn.* 1914.

Kathlyn Hare goes to India in search of her father Colonel Hare, who has disappeared after being named heir to an Indian kingdom. The villain Umballa has put the colonel in prison and plans to take over the country by marrying Kathlyn after she is crowned queen as her father's heir. Kathlyn undergoes a series of harrowing adventures while she resists marrying Umballa and tries to find her father. She is rescued frequently by white hunter John Bruce. In the end, her father is freed; Umballa is killed; and Kathlyn and Bruce are wed.

McHenry, James. *The Betrothed of Wyoming.* 1830.

Settlers in the territory near the Susquehanna River welcome the Austin family in 1776. The Austin party had rescued Mary Watson and Agnes Norwood from Indians. Agnes and Henry Austin become engaged. Also in the party is Tory renegade John Butler, loved by Isabella Austin who rescued him from prison. The turmoil of the Revolutionary War comes to the settlement. Henry joins the colonials while Butler continues his guerilla activities. Isabella goes insane because Butler rejects her, and she is killed during a battle. Henry arrives with the militia just as Butler is about to kill Agnes' father and friends.

Major, Charles. *When Knighthood Was in Flower.* 1898.

Princess Mary, sister of Henry VIII, falls in love with Charles Brandon, a captain of the guard. They elope but are captured, and Brandon is sentenced to die. In order to save him, Mary agrees to marry aging Louis XII of France. She wears out the old king with strenuous activities and long hours. When he dies, Mary is free to marry Brandon.

Page, Thomas Nelson. *Gordon Keith.* 1903.

Gordon Keith is the son of Southern General Keith. After

the war, the family has lost all its money, and Gordon becomes a teacher. He falls in love with Alice Yorke, but her mother opposes the match because of Gordon's poverty and takes Alice to New York. Gordon rises to being a successful engineer, but Alice has married a wealthy, older man. She and Gordon remain friends. Although Alice later becomes a widow, she and Gordon never resume their romance. Gordon becomes a wealthy mine owner and finally falls in love with Lois Huntington whose father bought the Keith plantation. The two wed after Gordon has prevented panic in banking circles.

Paulding, James Kirke. *The Dutchman's Fireside.* 1831.

Sybrandt Westbrook loves his aristocratic cousin Catalina Vancour. After he rescues her from drowning and from a renegade Indian, Catalina returns his love. In spite of her mother's opposition, Catalina remains true to Sybrandt who becomes a scout for Sir William Johnson in the French and Indian War. Sybrandt is reported killed in battle. His unexpected return, wounded but not dead, is cause for joy, and he and Catalina marry.

Read, Martha. *Monima or The Beggar Girl.* 1802.

Monima Fontanbleu works as a seamstress to support herself and her aged father. She cannot find enough work and they are close to starving. Madame Sontine is jealous of Monima's beauty and exerts great effort to destroy her by putting her in the poorhouse or shipping her to Africa. Monsieur Sontine, however, continually rescues Monima from his wife's perfidy. Finally, Madame dies, and Monima weds Monsieur Sontine.

Roe, Edward Payson. *Barriers Burned Away.* 1872.

Dennis Fleet must support his two sisters and mother after the death of his father. He goes to work in an art gallery as a porter and, through hard work, rises to chief clerk. He falls in love with the owner's daughter, Christine Ludolph. However, Christine rejects him because of the difference in their social classes. Further, she is not an active Christian as he is. During the great Chicago fire, Dennis rescues her, and she accepts the Christian faith. Dennis is now a famous artist, and the two are wed.

Roe, Edward Payson. *Without a Home.* 1881.

The Jocelyn family goes from wealth to poverty as Mr. Jocelyn's business fails and he becomes addicted to morphine. Mildred Jocelyn is loved by Roger Atwood, a young man from the country trying to make his way in the city. In spite of her family's poverty, Mildred remains conscious of Roger's uncultured background, and she cannot accept him. Even when he rescues her from a jail sentence by clearing her of a charge of theft, Mildred can feel only gratitude. She becomes a nurse. When Roger, now a rich lawyer, is hurt while stopping a runaway carriage, Mildred realizes that she loves him, and they are wed.

Rowson, Susanna. *Reuben and Rachel or Tales of Old Times.* 1798.

The adventures of a family are traced from the fifteenth century in Wales to the eighteenth century in America. The final episode deals with the twins Reuben and Rachel. Rachel marries secretly to protect her husband's fortune. When he goes off to America, she follows and at last they are able to live as man and wife. Meanwhile, Reuben has been searching for proof that he is the heir to an American estate. He is captured by Indians. The daughter of the chief falls in love with him and rescues him, leading him to civilization. Reuben discovers the proof he needs to claim the estate, weds an English girl, and the Indian maiden commits suicide. Reuben and Rachel, however, are happy in the new world.

Sedgwick, Catherine M. *Hope Leslie or Early Times in The Massachusetts.* 1827.

William Fletcher takes his two orphaned nieces, Hope and Faith Leslie, to his home in New England. There is an Indian raid and Everell Fletcher and Faith Leslie are taken captive. Through the intervention of the chief's daughter, Magawisca, who loves him, Everell escapes, but Faith remains a prisoner and eventually marries an Indian. After living in England for seven years, Everell returns to New England. He is in love with Hope Leslie although he is engaged to Esther Downing. Magawisca is arrested and tried as a witch. Everell and Hope manage to rescue her from jail, and she goes away, still in love with Everell. Esther releases Everell, and he and Hope marry.

Simms, William Gilmore. *The Yemassee.* 1835.

Lord Charles Craven, governor of Carolina, is posing as cavalier Captain Gabriel Harrison in order to investigate potential Indian uprisings. He is in love with Bess Matthews, but her father opposes the match. After Craven rescues Bess from a pirate, her father consents to their marriage. Craven reveals his identity, and the couple are wed.

Southworth, E.D.E.N. *Ishmael or In the Depths.* 1864.

Ishmael Worth is believed to be illegitimate because his mother died without revealing her secret marriage to wealthy Herman Brudenell, who has gone to Europe. As a youth, Ishmael rescues the two sons of James Middleton from a fire and is rewarded with an education, which starts him on the way to success. Ishmael falls in love with rich Claudia Merlin, who loves him but will not consider marriage to anyone who is socially beneath her. Ishmael becomes a lawyer, and Claudia marries Lord Vincent. In the sequel, *Self-Raised or From the Depths* (1876), Ishmael's real parentage is revealed, and he rescues Claudia from her husband's plot to kill her. However, Ishmael no longer loves Claudia, and she bitterly regrets her mistake.

Southworth, E.D.E.N. *The Three Beauties, or Shannondale.* 1851.

In the Shenandoah Valley, widow Margery Summerfield lives with her daughter Imogene and niece Winny Darling. Winny is in love with her tutor Edgar Ardenne. They elope, but they sink into poverty and finally starvation. Edgar leaves, and Winny returns to Imogene with her baby daughter. Imogene is unhappy because she has fallen in love with the priest, Father Vellemont. Finally, matters are straightened out. Edgar returns to Winny, and Father Vellemont is released from his vows to marry Imogene.

Stephens, Mrs. Anna Sophia. *Malaeska; The Indian Wife of the White Hunter.* 1860.

Malaeska is married to William Danforth, who deserts her after she saves him from Indians. Later, she finds him dying after an Indian battle. He tells her to take their son to his parents in Manhattan. The grandparents welcome their grandson but insist that Malaeska conceal the fact that she is the mother and act as a servant in the house. After several years, Malaeska flees with her son to the woods, intending to return to her people. The boy, however, wishes to return to his grandfather, and she allows the grandfather to take him away from her. She spends the rest of her life living on the edge of white civilization. When she meets her grown son at last, she tells him that she is his mother. Horrified, he commits suicide, and Malaeska dies on his grave.

Tourgée, Albion W. *A Fool's Errand.* 1879.
Comfort Servosse moves to North Carolina after the Civil War and buys a plantation. As an ex-Union officer and an active Republican, Servosse makes many enemies. His daughter, Lily, falls in love with Melville Gurney, a Southerner. Both families oppose the match. After Melville helps Lily rescue her father from a Klan ambush, Servosse withdraws his objections to the marriage. Melville's father, however, does not consent to the marriage until a year later when Servosse dies.

Twain, Mark. *The Adventures of Tom Sawyer.* 1876.
Tom Sawyer, a young boy in a Missouri town near the Mississippi River, lives with his Aunt Polly. Tom has a variety of adventures with his friend Huckleberry Finn. Tom and Huck see Injun Joe kill the town doctor, and they tell the authorities. While on a school picnic, Tom and Becky Thatcher are lost in a cave where Tom sees Injun Joe's hideout. Tom and Becky are rescued, but Injun Joe dies in the cave. Huck is taken in by the Widow Douglas.

Webster, Jean. *Daddy-Long-Legs.* 1912.
Jerusha Abbott, the oldest orphan in the orphanage, is sent to college by a trustee who wishes to remain anonymous. He only requires that Jerusha write to him once a month about her progress. Jerusha does well at college. She meets Jervis Pendleton, her roommate's uncle, and he becomes very important to her. Jerusha begins to write fiction and sells a story. She wins a scholarship and pays her own way at school. By the time she graduates from college, she is writing a novel. Jervis proposes and reveals that he is her benefactor. The two are wed.

White, Stewart Edward. *The Silent Places.* 1904.

Dick Herron and old Sam Bolton are sent by Hudson Bay Company to catch a renegade Indian who has not paid for his outfit. Before they leave the fort, Dick pays some compliments to an Indian girl, May-may-gwan, who falls in love with him and follows the men through the wilderness. The men cannot make her turn back. Although she helps them find the renegade's trail and does the chores, Dick is abusive and hostile to her. Finally, they are without food. May-may-gwan dies in the snow from starvation just as the renegade Indian staggers up snowblind. Dick and old Sam make it back to the fort and are hailed as heroes.

Wilson, Augusta Evans. *Beulah.* 1859.

Beulah Benton and her sister Lilly are orphans. Lilly is adopted, but Beulah is hired out as a nursemaid. When Lilly dies of scarlet fever, Dr. Guy Hartwell is so touched by Beulah's grief that he takes the girl in and gives her an education. Beulah becomes a teacher and insists on supporting herself instead of living an idle life as Hartwell wishes her to. She becomes a famous writer, and in the end agrees to marry Hartwell, who has declared his love.

Wilson, Augusta Evans. *St. Elmo.* 1867.

Orphan Edna Earl is on her way to find work in a factory in Columbus, Georgia, when there is a train wreck, and she is injured. Mrs. Murray, a wealthy widow, takes her in and offers to give her an education. Mrs. Murray's son is the dissipated and brooding St. Elmo. Edna studies and develops into a religious scholar. She and St. Elmo have long philosophical discussions about religion. Edna writes scholarly works and gains an international reputation. She refuses to marry St. Elmo until he reforms. He finally becomes a minister and they marry.

Wister, Owen. *The Virginian.* 1902.

Schoolteacher Molly Stark Wood comes to Wyoming and meets the exciting cowboy called the Virginian. While the hero deals with local rustlers and evil men, Molly decides that she can never love a man who is socially beneath her. When she rescues the Virginian from an Indian attack and nurses him back to health, however, Molly comes to appreciate his natural heroism and innate moral strength. After a shootout with the villain Trampas, the Virginian and the schoolteacher marry.

Woodworth, Samuel. *The Champions of Freedom, or The Mysterious Chief: A Romance of the Nineteenth Century Founded on the Events of the War Between the United States and Great Britain which terminated in March, 1815.* 1816.

Major Willoughby lives near Lake Erie in 1809 with his son George and daughter Amelia. George is in love with their neighbor Catherine Fleming. He goes to Harvard to study and makes the acquaintance of Thomas Sandford, a dissipated young man. George rejects a life of dissipation. Angry, Sandford tries to seduce Catherine as revenge. After many harrowing episodes, Sandford is killed, and Catherine and George are reunited.

Wright, Caleb. *Wyoming, A Tale.* 1845.

Pioneers in northern Pennsylvania rescue an Indian boy from accidental hanging. The boy, called Hanger, stays with the John Henderson family for a while and then leaves. Ten years later in 1775, the family is torn apart when Walter Henderson joins the colonials and Charles Henderson joins the British. Walter loves Ruth Dinning, the daughter of a Tory. When Walter is captured by Mohawks, he is saved from death by a renowned chief, who reveals he was the boy called Hanger. After being a prisoner of the British and escaping, Walter is reunited with Ruth at the close of the war.

Wright, Harold Bell. *That Printer of Udell's.* 1903.

Dick Falkner, a young printer, gets a job at George Udell's shop after virtually every solid citizen and Christian in town has turned him down. Dick has been dissipated in the past but knows now that Christianity is the best way to live. He loves Amy Goodrich, daughter of a rich storeowner. Amy is forbidden to see Dick because he is socially beneath her. She runs away to the city but cannot take care of herself and ends up in a brothel. On her first night there, Dick arrives with a Salvation Army group and saves her from entering a life of sin. Amy's brother has developed gambling debts, and Dick saves him from disgrace. In spite of Dick's help, Amy's father still opposes the match. But the couple reject his authority and wed. Dick goes off to Washington as a congressman.

Wright, Harold Bell. *The Winning of Barbara Worth.* 1911.

While in the Colorado desert, banker Jefferson Worth rescues a little girl whose parents have died. Barbara grows up to be a charming and intelligent young lady. While her father is involved with business deals to develop the irrigation possibilities in the desert, Barbara falls in love with Willard Holmes, an engineer for the corrupt Eastern firm trying to cheat Jefferson Worth. After Willard proves his morality by rejecting the corrupt company and helping Barbara's father, he and Barbara can wed.

Notes

Chapter I

[1]James D. Hart, *The Popular Book* (1950; rpt. Berkeley, Calif.: Univ. of California Press, 1963), p. 93.

[2]Caroline Ticknor, *Hawthorne and His Publisher* (Boston: Houghton Mifflin Co., 1913), pp. 141-142.

[3]Russel Nye, *The Unembarrassed Muse: The Popular Arts in America* (New York: Dial Press, 1970), pp. 29-31.

[4]Abraham Kaplan, "The Aesthetics of the Popular Arts," *Journal of Aesthetics* (1964), p. 356.

[5]Hart, p. 285.

[6]Nye, p. 4.

[7]John Cawelti, "The Concept of Formula in the Study of Popular Literature," *Journal of Popular Culture,* 3 (1969), p. 388.

[8]Cawelti, p. 390.

[9]Quoted in Hart, p. 208.

[10]John Fox, Jr., *The Little Shepherd of Kingdom Come* (1903; rpt. New York: Grosset & Dunlap, n.d.), pp. 269-77. All further references to this work appear in the text.

[11]Beadle & Co., introd. *Malaeska; The Indian Wife of the White Hunter* by Ann Sophia Stephens (1860; rpt. New York: The John Day Co., 1929), n.p. All further references to this work appear in the text.

[12]Kaplan, p. 361.

Chapter II

[1]Augusta Evans Wilson, *Beulah* (1859; rpt. New York: Grosset & Dunlap, 1900), p. 43. All further references to this work appear in the text.

[2]Hart, p. 118.

[3]Augusta Evans Wilson, *St. Elmo* (1867, rpt. New York: Grosset & Dunlap, n.d.), p. 31. All further references to this work appear in the text.

[4]Maria Cummins, *The Lamplighter* (1854, rpt. London: George Routledge and Sons, Ltd., n.d.), p. 9. All further references to this work appear in the text.

[5]Jessee L. Holman, *The Prisoners of Niagara or Errors of Education* (Frankfort: William Gerard, 1810), p. 46. All further references to this work appear in the text.

[6]Caleb Wright, *Wyoming, a Tale* (New York: Harper & Brothers, 1845), p. 29. All further references to this work appear in the text.

[7]Hamlin Garland, *A Little Norsk or Old Pap's Flaxen* (New York: D. Appleton and Company, 1892), p. 10. All further references to this work appear in the text.

[8]William Lillibridge, *Ben Blair, The Story of a Plainsman* (Chicago: A.C. McClurg & Co., 1905), p. 32. All further references to this work appear in the text.

[9]Nye, p. 36.

[10]Irving Bacheller, *Eben Holden* (Boston: Lothrop Publishing Co., 1900), p. 8. All further references to this work appear in the text.

[11]Frank Luther Mott, *Golden Multitudes* (New York: Macmillan Co., 1947), p. 214.

[12]Jean Webster, *Daddy-Long-Legs* (1912, rpt. New York: The Century Co., 1915), p. 14. All further references to this work appear in the text.

[13]Josiah G. Holland, *Sevenoaks; a Story of Today* (1875; rpt. Upper Saddle River, New Jersey: The Gregg Press, 1968), p. 39. All further references to this work appear in the text.

[14]Mott, p. 232.

[15]Harold Bell Wright, *The Winning of Barbara Worth* (Chicago: The Book Supply Co., 1911), p. 43. All further references to this work appear in the text.

[16]Gertrude Atherton, *Patience Sparhawk and Her Times* (1895; rpt. Toronto: The Macmillan Co. of Canada, 1910). All further references to this work appear in the text.

[17]Louisa May Alcott, *Rose in Bloom* (1876; rpt. New York: Grosset & Dunlap, 1927), p. 242. All further references to this work appear in the text.

[18]E.D.E.N. Southworth, *Ishmael or In the Depths* (1864; rpt. New York: A.L. Burt Co., 19—), p. 203. All further references to this work appear in the text.

[19]Thomas Nelson Page, *Gordon Keith* (1903; rpt. New York: Charles Scribner's Sons, 1905), p. 481. All further references to this work appear in the text.

[20]Samuel Clemens, *The Adventures of Tom Sawyer* in *The Family Mark Twain* (1876; rpt. New York: Harper & Brothers Publishers, 1935), p. 433. All further references to this work appear in the text.

Chapter III

[1]Emerson Bennett, *The Forest Rose: A Tale of the Frontier* (1850; rpt. Athens, Ohio: Ohio University Press, 1973), p. 11. All further references to this work appear in the text.

[2]Martha Read, *Monima or The Begger Girl* (New York: printed by P.R. Johnson for I.N. Ralston, 1802), p. 227. All further references to this work appear in the text.

[3]James Kirke Paulding, *The Dutchman's Fireside* (1831; rpt. New Haven, Conn.: College & University Press, 1966), p. 64. All further references to this work appear in the text.

[4]Hart, p. 82, and Nye, p. 22.

[5]Mott, p. 74.

[6]James Fenimore Cooper, *The Last of the Mohicans* (1826; rpt. New York: New American Library, 1962), p. 132. All further references to this work appear in the text.

[7]William Gilmore Simms, *The Yemassee* (1835; rpt. Boston: Houghton Mifflin, Riverside Edition, 1961), p. 141. All further references to this work appear in the text.

[8]Hart, p. 199.

[9]Charles Major, *When Knighthood Was in Flower* (1898; rpt. New York Grosset and Dunlap, n.d.), p. 120. All further references to this work appear in the text.

[10]Mary Johnston, *To Have and To Hold* (Boston: Houghton Mifflin and Co., 1900), p. 21. All further references to this work appear in the text.

[11]Hart, p. 199.

[12]George Barr McCutcheon, *Beverly of Graustark* (1904; rpt. New York: Grosset and Dunlap, n.d.), p. 63. All further references to this work appear in the text.

[13]Owen Wister, *The Virginian* (1902; rpt. New York: The Macmillan Co., 1904), p. 101. All further references to this work appear in the text.

[14]Nye, p. 54. Nye cites Winston Churchill, Zane Grey, Harold Bell Wright, Gene Stratton-Porter, and Mary Roberts Rinehart as the most popular writers in the first quarter of the twentieth century.

[15]Zane Grey, *The Lone Star Ranger* (New York: Harper & Brothers 1914), p. 238. All further references to this work appear in the text.

[16]Albion W. Tourgée, *A Fool's Errand* (1879; rpt. New York: Harper & Row, 1966), p. 272. All further references to this work appear in the text.

[17]Hart, p. 121.

[18]Edward Payson Roe, *Barriers Burned Away* (1872; rpt. New York: Dodd, Mead & Co., 1892), p. 82. All further references to this work appear in the text.

[19]John Esten Cooke, *The Virginia Comedians or Old Days in the Old Dominion* (1854; rpt. New York: D. Appleton and Co., 1883), p. 87. All further references to this work appear in the text.

[20]Samuel Woodworth, *The Champions of Freedom, or The Mysterious Chief: A Romance of the Nineteenth Century founded on the Events of the War Between the United States and Great Britain which terminated in March, 1815,* 2nd ed (New York: Charles N. Baldwin, 1818), I, p. 182. All further references to this work appear in the text.

[21]Harold MacGrath, *The Adventures of Kathlyn* (Indianapolis: The Bobbs-Merrill Co., 1914), p. 94. All further references to this work appear in the text.

[22]William Dean Howells, *Indian Summer* (1886; rpt. Bloomington, Indiana; Indiana University Press, 1971), p. 253. All further references to this work appear in the text.

[23]Helen Andelin, *The Fascinating Girl* (Santa Barbara, Calif.: Pacific Press Santa Barbara, 1969), p. 295.

Chapter IV

[1]William Charvat, "Literature as Business," in *Literary History of the United States: History,* ed. Robert E. Spiller, et al. (London: The Macmillan Co., 1963), p. 956.

[2]John Cawelti, *Adventure, Mystery, and Romance* (Chicago: Univ. of Chicago Press, 1976), p. 278.

[3]Margaret Fuller Ossoli, *Woman in the Nineteenth Century and Kindred Papers Relating to the Sphere, Condition and Duties of Woman,* ed. Arthur B.

Fuller (Boston: Roberts Brothers, 1874), p. 119.

[4]Ossoli, p. 121.

[5]Ossoli, pp. 176-77.

[6]Margaret Deland, *The Rising Tide* (New York: Harper & Brothers Publishers, 1916), p. 141. All further references to this work appear in the text.

[7]George Washington Cable, *The Grandissimes* (1880; rpt. New York: Hill and Wang, 1957), p. 131. All further references to this work appear in the text.

[8]Edward Payson Roe, *Without a Home.* Vol. II of *The Works of E.P. Roe* (1881; rpt. New York: P. F. Collier & Son, 1902), p. 90. All further references to this work appear in the text.

[9]James Oliver Curwood, *God's Country and the Woman* (1914; rpt. New York: A.L. Burt Co., n.d.), p. 21. All further references to this work appear in the text.

[10]Harold Bell Wright, *That Printer of Udell's* (New York: A.L. Burt Co., 1903), p. 109. All further references to this work appear in the text.

[11]Cawelti, *Adventure,* p. 278.

[12]William Dean Howells, *Dr. Breen's Practice* (Boston: Houghton Mifflin Co., 1881), p. 15. All further references to this work appear in the text.

[13]Henry James, *The Bostonians* (1886; rpt. New York: The Modern Library, 1956), p. 18. All further references to this work appear in the text.

Chapter V

[1]Leslie A. Fiedler, *The Return of the Vanishing American* (New York: Stein and Day, 1968), pp. 50-51. Fiedler cites four myths as the foundation of the American concept of the West: *The Myth of Love in the Woods, The Myth of the White Woman with a Tomahawk, The Myth of the Good Companions in the Wilderness,* and *The Myth of the Runaway Male.*

[2]Fiedler, p. 64.

[3]Fiedler, p. 70

[4]Susanna Rowson, *Reuben and Rachel or Tales of Old Times* (Boston: Manning & Loring, 1798), II, p. 346. All further references to this work appear in the text.

[5]Mott, p. 142.

[6]E.D.E.N. Southworth, *The Three Beauties, or Shannondale* (1851: rpt. New York: Hurst & Co., n.d.), p. 27. All further references to this work appear in the text.

[7]Helen Waite Papashvily, *All The Happy Endings* (New York: Harper & Brothers Publishers, 1956), p. 41.

[8]Catherine M. Sedgwick, *Hope Leslie or Early Times in The Massachusetts* (1827; rpt. New York: Harper & Brothers, Publishers, 1855), I, p. 136. All further references to this work appear in the text.

[9]Jack London, *Smoke Bellew* (New York: The Century Co., 1912), p. 343. All further references to this work appear in the text.

[10]Stewart Edward White, *The Silent Places* (New York: McClure, Phillips & Co., 1904), p. 97. All further references to this work appear in the text.

[11]Basil King, *The Wild Olive* (New York: Harper & Brothers, 1910), p. 31. All further references to this work appear in the text.

¹²George Barr McCutcheon, *Jane Cable* (New York: Dodd, Mead & Co., 1906), p. 254. All further references to this work appear in the text.

¹³Oliver Wendell Holmes, *A Mortal Antipathy* (1885; rpt. Boston Houghton Mifflin and Co., 1892), p. 41. All further references to this work appear in the text. Holmes' primary concern in this novel was human psychology and unorthodox ways to solve psychological problems. Although Holmes probably was not interested in traditional male-female relationships, his novel is useful here because it uses the pattern of the physical rescue with role reversal. The awkwardness of such a role reversal is evident in the characterizations of the hero and heroine.

¹⁴Robert Montgomery Bird, *The Hawks of Hawk-Hollow* (Philadelphia: Carey, Lea, & Blanchard, 1835), I, p. 100. All further references to this work appear in the text.

Chapter VI

¹Hart, p. 285.
²Hart, p. 285.
³Cawelti, *Adventure,* p. 300.
⁴Fiedler, p. 77.

Bibliography
Novels

Alcott, Louisa May. *Rose in Bloom*. 1876; rpt. New York: Grossett & Dunlap, 1927.

Atherton, Gertrude, *Patience Sparhawk and Her Times*. 1895; rpt. Toronto: The Macmillan Co. of Canada, Ltd., 1910.

Bacheller, Irving. *Eben Holden*. Boston: Lothrop Publishing Co., 1900.

Bennett, Emerson. *The Forest Rose; A Tale of the Frontier*. 1885; rpt. Athens, Ohio: Ohio Univ. Press, 1973.

Bird, Robert Montgomery. *The Hawks of Hawk-Hollow*. 2 vols. Philadelphia: Carey, Lea, & Blanchard, 1835.

Cable, George Washington. *The Grandissimes*. 1880; rpt. New York: Hill and Wang, 1957.

Cooke, John Esten. *The Virginia Comedians or Old Days in the Old Dominion*. 1854; rpt. New York: D. Appleton and Co., 1883.

Cooper, James Fenimore. *The Last of the Mohicans*. 1826; rpt. New York: New American Library, 1962.

Cummins, Maria. *The Lamplighter*. 1854; rpt. London: George Routledge and Sons, ltd., n.d.

Curwood, James Oliver. *God's Country and the Woman*. 1914; rpt. New York: A.L. Burt Co., n.d.

Deland, Margaret. *The Rising Tide*. New York: Harper & Brothers, 1916.

Fox, John Jr. *The Little Shepherd of Kingdom Come*. 1903; rpt. New York: Grosset & Dunlap, n.d.

Garland, Hamlin. *A Little Norsk or Ol' Pap's Flaxen*. New York: D. Appleton and Co., 1892.

Grey, Zane. *The Lone Star Ranger*. New York: Harper & Brothers, 1914.

Holland, Josiah G. *Sevenoaks; a Story of Today*. 1875; rpt. Upper Saddle River, New Jersey: The Gregg Press, 1968.

Holman, Jessee L. *The Prisoners of Niagara or Errors of Education*. Frankfort: William Girard, 1810.

Holmes, Oliver Wendell. *A Mortal Antipathy*. 1885; rpt. Boston: Houghton Mifflin and Co., 1892.

Howells, William Dean. *Dr. Breen's Practice*. Boston: Houghton Mifflin Co., 1881.

———. *Indian Summer*. 1886; rpt. Bloomington, Indiana: Indiana Univ. Press, 1971.

James, Henry. *The Bostonians*. 1886; rpt. New York: The Modern Library, 1956.

Johnston, Mary. *To Have and To Hold*. Boston: Houghton, Mifflin and Co., 1900.

King, Basil. *The Wild Olive*. New York: Harper & Brothers, 1910.

Lillibridge, William. *Ben Blair, The Story of a Plainsman.* 5th ed. Chicago: A.C. McClurg & Co., 1905.

London, Jack. *Smoke Bellew.* New York: The Century Co., 1912.

McCutcheon, George Barr. *Beverly of Graustark.* 1904; rpt. New York: Grosset & Dunlap, n.d.

―――― *Jane Cable.* New York: Dodd, Mead & Co., 1906.

MacGrath, Harold. *The Adventures of Kathlyn.* Indianapolis: The Bobbs-Merrill Co., 1914.

McHenry, James. *The Betrothed of Wyoming.* 2nd ed. Philadelphia: principal booksellers, 1830.

Major, Charles. *When Knighthood Was in Flower.* 1898; rpt. New York: Grosset & Dunlap, n.d.

Page, Thomas Nelson. *Gordon Keith.* 1903; rpt. New York: Charles Scribner's Sons, 1905.

Paulding, James Kirke. *The Dutchman's Fireside.* 1831; rpt. New Haven, Conn.: College & Univ. Press, 1966.

Read, Martha. *Monima or The Beggar Girl.* New York: printed by P.R. Johnson for I.N. Ralston, 1802.

Roe, Edward Payson. *Barriers Burned Away.* 1872; rpt. New York: Dodd, Mead & Co., 1892.

―――― *Without a Home* in *The Works of E.P. Roe.* 1881; rpt. New York: P.F. Collier & Son, 1902.

Rowson, Susanna. *Reuben and Rachel or Tales of Old Times.* 2 vols. Boston: Manning & Loring, 1798.

Sedgwick, Catherine M. *Hope Leslie or Early Times in The Massachusetts.* 1827; rpt. New York: Harper & Brothers Publishers, 1855.

Simms, William Gilmore. *The Yemassee.* 1835; rpt. Boston: Houghton Mifflin, 1961.

Southworth, E.D.E.N. *Ishmael or In the Depths.* 1864; rpt. New York: A.L. Burt Co., 19-.

―――― *The Three Beauties or Shannondale.* 1851; rpt. New York: Hurst & Co., n.d.

Stephens, Mrs. Ann Sophia. *Malaeska; The Indian Wife of the White Hunter.* 1860; rpt. New York: The John Day Co., 1929.

Tourgée, Albion W. *A Fool's Errand.* 1880; rpt. New York: Harper & Row Publishers, 1966.

Twain, Mark. *The Adventures of Tom Sawyer* in *The Family Mark Twain.* 1876; rpt. New York: Harper & Brothers Publishers, 1935.

Webster, Jean. *Daddy-Long-Legs.* 1912; rpt. New York: The Century Co., 1915.

White, Stewart Edward. *The Silent Places.* New York: McClure, Phillips & Co., 1904.

Wilson, Augusta Evans. *Beulah.* 1859; rpt. New York: Grosset & Dunlap, 1900.

―――― *St. Elmo.* 1867; rpt. New York: Grosset & Dunlap, n.d.

Wister, Owen. *The Virginian.* 1902; rpt. New York: The Macmillan Co., 1904.

Woodworth, Samuel. *The Champions of Freedom, or The Mysterious Chief: A Romance of the Nineteenth Century Founded on the Events of the War Between the United States and Great Britain which terminated in March, 1815.* 2 vols. 2nd ed. New York: Charles N. Baldwin, 1818.

Wright, Caleb. *Wyoming, A Tale.* New York: Harper & Brothers, 1845.
Wright, Harold Bell. *That Printer of Udell's.* New York: A.L. Burt Co., 1903.
_____ *The Winning of Barbara Worth.* Chicago: The Book Supply Co., 1911.

Critical Sources

Andelin, Helen. *The Fascinating Girl.* Santa Barbara, Calif.: Pacific Press Santa Barbara, 1969.

Benschoten, Virginia van. "Changes in Best Sellers Since World War One." *Journal of Popular Culture,* I, No. 4 (1968), 379-388.

Bode, Carl. *The Anatomy of American Popular Culture 1840-1861.* Berkeley: Univ. of California Press, 1959.

Bristed, John. *The Resources of the United States of America.* New York: James Eastburn & Co., 1818.

Brown, Herbert Ross. *The Sentimental Novel in America 1789-1860.* Durham, N.C.: Duke Univ. Press, 1940.

Browne, Ray B., Marshall Fishwick, and Michael T. Marsden. *Heroes of Popular Culture.* Bowling Green, Ohio: Bowling Green Univ. Popular Press, 1972.

Cawelti, John F. *Adventure, Mystery, and Romance.* Chicago: Univ. of Chicago Press, 1976.

_____."The Concept of Formula in the Study of Popular Literature." *Journal of Popular Culture,* 3 No. 3 (1969), 381-390.

_____. "Notes Toward an Aesthetic of Popular Culture." *Journal of Popular Culture,* 5, No. 2 (1971), 255-268.

Charvat, William. "Literature as Business," in *Literary History of the United States: History.* ed. Robert E. Spiller, et al. 3rd ed. London: The Macmillan Co., 1963.

Cowie, Alexander. *The Rise of the American Novel.* New York: American Book Co., 1948.

_____. "The Vogue of the Domestic Novel 1850-1870." The *South Atlantic Quarterly,* 51, No. 4 (1942), 416-424.

Fiedler, Leslie A. *Love and Death in the American Novel.* New York: Dell Publishing Co., 1969.

_____. *The Return of the Vanishing American.* New York: Stein and Day, 1968.

Fishwick, Marshall and Ray B. Browne, eds. *Icons of Popular Culture.* Bowling Green, Ohio Bowling Green Univ. Popular Press, 1970.

Gans, Herbert J. *Popular Culture and High Culture: An Analysis and Evaluation of Taste.* New York: Basic Books, 1974.

Garrison, Dee. "Immoral Fiction in the Late Victorian Library." *American Quarterly,* 28, No. 1 (1976), 71-89.

Gowans, Alan. *The Unchanging Arts: New Forms for the Traditional Function of Art in Society.* Philadelphia: J.B. Lippincott Co., 1971.

Hackett, Alice Payne. *Fifty Years of Best Sellers, 1895-1945.* New York: R.R. Bowker Co., 1945.

Hammel, William M., ed. *The Popular Arts in America.* 2nd ed. New York: Harcourt Brace Jovanovich, 1977.

Hart, James D. *The Popular Book.* 1950; rpt. Berkeley: Univ. of California Press, 1963.

Hockey, Dorothy C. "The Good and the Beautiful, A Study of Best

Selling Novels in America, 1895-1920." Diss. Case Western Reserve, 1947.

Hofstadter, Beatrice K. "Popular Culture and the Romantic Heroine." *The American Scholar*, 30, No. 1 (1960-61), 98-116.

Kaplan, Abraham. "The Aesthetics of the Popular Arts." *Journal of Aesthetics* (1964), 351-364.

Loshe, Lillie Deming. *The Early American Novel.* New York: Columbia Univ. Press, 1907.

Madden, David. "The Necessity for an Aesthetics of Popular Culture." *Journal of Popular Culture,* 7 (1973), 1-13.

Mott, Frank Luther. *Golden Multitudes.* New York: Macmillan Co., 1947.

The National Union Catalog Pre-1956 Imprints. London: Mansell, 1974.

Nye, Russel. *The Unembarrassed Muse: The Popular Arts in America.* New York: The Dial Press, 1970.

Orians, G. Harrison. "The Censure of Fiction in American Romances and Magazines 1789-1810." *PMLA,* 52, No. 1 (1937), 195-214.

Ossoli, Margaret Fuller. *Woman in the Nineteenth Century and Kindred Papers Relating to the Sphere, Condition, and Duties of Woman.* ed. Arthur B. Fuller. Boston: Roberts Brothers, 1874.

Papashvily, Helen Waite. *All The Happy Endings.* New York: Harper & Brothers Publishers, 1956.

Perkins, Frederic C. "Free Libraries & Unclean Books." *Library Journal* 10, No. 12 (1885), 396-399.

Petter, Henri. *The Early American Novel.* Columbus, Ohio Ohio State Univ. Press, 1971.

Reynolds, Quentin. *The Fiction Factory, or From Pulp Row to Quality Street.* New York: Random House, 1955.

Rosenberg, Bernard and David Manning White, eds. *Mass Culture: The Popular Arts in America.* Glencoe, Ill.: The Free Press, 1957.

Satterwhite, Joseph N. "The Tremulous Formula: Form and Technique in *Godey's* Fiction." *American Quarterly,* 8, No. 2, (1956), 99-113.

Smith, Henry Nash. "The Scribbling Women and the Cosmic Success Story." *Critical Inquiry* 1, No. 1 (1974), 47-70.

Van Doren, Carl. *The American Novel 1789-1939.* New York: The Macmillan Co., 1940.

Wasserstrom, William. *Heiress of All the Ages: Sex and Sentiment in the Genteel Tradition.* Minneapolis: Univ. of Minnesota Press, 1959.

Western, Richard D. "Genres & Teaching: Uses of Formula Fiction." MMLA Convention, St. Louis. 5 Nov. 1976.

Ziff, Larzer. *The American 1890s, Life & Times of a Lost Generation.* New York: Viking Press, 1966.

Index